A Different Kind of Cell

Clayton Fountain

A Different Kind of Cell

The Story of a Murderer
Who Became a Monk

W. PAUL JONES

William B. Eerdmans Publishing Company
Grand Rapids, Michigan / Cambridge, U.K.

Published 2011 by

Wm. B. Eerdmans Publishing Co.

2140 Oak Industrial Drive N.E., Grand Rapids, Michigan 49505 /
P.O. Box 163, Cambridge CB3 9PU U.K.

Printed in the United States of America

17 16 15 14 13 12 11   7 6 5 4 3 2 1

Library of Congress Cataloging-in-Publication Data

Jones, W. Paul (William Paul)

A different kind of cell: the story of a murderer who became a monk /
W. Paul Jones.

p.   cm.

ISBN 978-0-8028-6651-6 (pbk.: alk. paper)

1. Fountain, Clayton Anthony, 1955-2004. 2. Catholic converts —
United States — Biography. 3. Murderers — United States —
Biography. 4. Monks — United States — Biography.   I. Title.

BX4668.F66P38   2011

282.092 — dc22

[B]

2011007215

www.eerdmans.com

For the thousands of persons
on death rows
everywhere,
whom the justice system in our name
has placed beyond our mercy —
assuming
that they are
beyond
the transforming
Mercy of God.

Contents

Foreword

———————

Father Paul has brought forth this important book, *A Different Kind of Cell,* which presents what may be the most powerful case of all against the death penalty. What he unfolds for us is the story of a man — Clayton Fountain — purported to be the most violent criminal with which our country's federal system has ever had to deal. Totally guilty of his multiple crimes, he proudly confessed five brutal and intentional murders. With four of them done within the walls of this country's highest-security prison, he was declared so incorrigible and ruthlessly dangerous that a special escape-proof isolation cell was constructed for him within a wing reserved for the criminally insane. Once he was locked permanently within it, the expectation was that he would experience the ultimate penalty worse than death. Cut off from all human contact, he was left to self-destruct.

In a strange unfolding, Father Paul was drawn toward this man as opportunities slowly invited a relationship. In a manner defying all logic and expectations, a transformation began happening in that remote concrete-and-metal vault. The power of this book is the way in which it makes an undeniable witness that no one is beyond the reach of God to restore health and sanity — humanness.

The divine mercy is always available, and conversion is never impossible. If so, then every person executed, even if totally guilty of the most violent of crimes, is a child of God who is being snuffed out before God is through working with him. The words of Clayton Fountain himself, made clarion in this book, need to be heard widely; they tug at the moral foundation of all religions and the decency of every citizen. If this man can be redeemed, then no one is beyond the mercy of God. No one. The message of this book is that to kill anyone on the assumption that their redemption is impossible is to take the place of God.

Father W. Paul Jones writes this story from multiple perspectives. He was an ordained United Methodist minister for over forty years; he is now a Roman Catholic priest, a Family Brother of a monastery of the Cistercian Order of the Strict Observance, and a spiritual director with the Hermitage Spiritual Retreat Center. He spent his professional life mainly as a university and seminary professor of theology. Then he encountered Clayton Fountain. And now, in these pages, he and his amazing story *encounter you.*

SISTER HELEN PREJEAN
Author of *Dead Man Walking*
and *Death of Innocents*

Prologue: On Mercy

M ost of us believe in forgiveness — especially if it has to do with us personally in regard to something we have done. It's possible for us to be a bit more expansive in extending forgiveness to our family or close friends — if they apologize first. But when it comes to persons more remote, we begin to reference circumstances and conditions that push them outside the realm of forgiveness. And when the issue becomes deadly acts of violence, our natural response is to conclude that under certain circumstances the supreme punishment of death is justifiable. "An eye for an eye and a tooth for a tooth."

The story of Clayton A. Fountain became for me an intense, uninvited personal testing of such conditions. There were five violent killings and a brutal record of pain and injury left in his path. Doesn't that justify the supreme punishment?

Understandably, prison authorities regarded Clayton as the most dangerous human being in the whole federal system. In fact, his behavior in multiple prisons was such that they were forced to take the drastic measure of sealing him off from almost all human contact, condemning him for the rest of his life to solitary confinement in a specially constructed chamber.

Through a strange series of circumstances, I was drawn into his life, becoming in time his spiritual director and eventually his friend. On one thing there was agreement by everyone who was in any way involved: the behavioral turnaround in Clayton's life was an incredible one. Through letters, phone calls, and personal visits, I became part of his pilgrimage and one of the few persons who dared to believe that what was happening was authentic.

As a Christian, I found myself in a process that raised for me one of the most fundamental of questions. Are there persons who have so squandered their humanity that Divine Mercy abandons them? If so, does it not follow that because they are outside of God's willingness and/or ability to restore them to simple decency, execution is the just conclusion? I once thought so. Then I entered the Clayton Fountain story.

The content of this book is largely the result of my personal contacts with Clayton Fountain over a six-year period, involving numerous visits, phone calls, and letters. In addition, I have been privileged to read Clayton's correspondence to and from other persons, interview others who have had personal contact with him, relate with members of his family, gain access to prison records, and read related newspaper articles. It is impossible to sort through such experiences and materials without having a point of view. Although mine evolved as my involvement grew, threads of my perspective must somehow include the fact that I am a retired professor of theology, a Family Brother of Assumption Abbey, a monastery of the Order of Cistercians of the Strict Observance (Trappist), a hermit, and a Roman Catholic priest who was raised in Appalachia as a Protestant and ordained as a United Methodist minister. In a word, I am perhaps as strange as the person this story tries to understand.

CHAPTER ONE

An Overture

While I have always tended to find God's leadings of me inexplicable, one relationship in particular defies all logic. There is no conceivable way I could have imagined that I would become the closest friend of Clayton Anthony Fountain — the legendary killer, widely regarded as the most dangerous person in the entire U.S. federal prison system.

The simple facts are indisputable. He was a hardened killer, convicted of murdering in cold blood five different people at five different times with no apparent motive. In fact, four of his five victims were in prison with him in the United States Penitentiary in Marion, Illinois — the successor to Alcatraz. Although constrained in the cell block of "last resort" in this highest of security prisons, given a single cell inside a "cage" designed to enforce severe isolation and extraordinary surveillance, Clayton earned in just seven years a fearsome renown of being both incorrigible and uncontrollable. Of him, U.S. prosecuting attorney Frederick Hess alleged, "I have never, in eighteen years of law practice, ever found a cold-stone killer that deserves the death penalty more than he does."

Yet at the time of Clayton's rampages, there was no death penalty for federal prisoners — not yet. Thus officials were baffled at the same time that they were desperate for some solution to "the Fountain nightmare." Much to the relief of everyone at Marion, it was decided in 1984 that there was no other alternative but to construct an extraordinary chamber in the bowels of the Medical Center for Federal Prisoners in Springfield, Missouri, so designed that Clayton could be totally isolated, once and for all. There he would remain in solitary confinement until he died twenty-one years later. The intention was to cut him off completely from all contact with other humans — except for guards, carefully chosen.

Disdain for him was so heavy for a number of years that the silent treatment was complete, without even a word from the guard who would slide Clayton's meals through a slot in the double-plated steel door. Especially infuriating for the federal prison personnel was that Clayton had intentionally stabbed to death a prison guard in Marion and severely wounded two others. The unspoken working assumption seemed to be that forcing an inevitable nervous breakdown would be just retribution for Clayton. Indeed, years later, when I was finally permitted to visit Clayton, his isolation chamber was across the corridor from a double-tiered unit for the criminally insane. A mélange of screams issuing from their padded cells provided the only "human" sounds Clayton could hear. Not even his mother, Ruth, doubted the appropriateness of Clayton's imprisonment, yet she never gave up praying for her son, plagued by the nightmare that the authorities had "thrown away the key."

What was to unfold within that isolation chamber, however, would be contrary to every expectation — incredibly so. Yet I must be clear from the beginning of this story that only a very few of us would ever come to believe, at least publicly, the authenticity of what was to happen. A staff member of the chaplain's office made a comment to me that perhaps spoke for many: "The fact that he hasn't become unglued under such conditions only proves how crazy the man is. A sane person would have been a basket case long before this." Reactions to his changed behavior, then, were mixed. On the one hand, there were federal prison authorities who admitted surprise at his change without trusting that it would last. On the other hand, there were those who regarded what they were observing as one of the biggest con jobs in prison history. The most kindly judgment available was that Clayton was "self-deceived."

Whatever conclusion one comes to draw, there is agreement on one thing: something intriguing did happen over the fifteen-year period beginning in December 1989. Still, whatever the authenticity, a "catch-22" was destined always to circumscribe it. One of Clayton's few parole-board reviews expressed it this way: "Parole cannot even be considered unless Clayton's self-professed transformation could be tested through social interaction with other persons." Yet, understandably, the prison authorities prohibited anyone even to touch Clayton, certainly in no way daring to gamble on opening his double steel door to permit his interacting with anyone. Thus, as we shall see, any talk of parole would prove to be little more than theoretical, for what board would entertain release for a prisoner whose trail of sentencing had accumulated five life sentences to be lived out consecutively? Through it all, however, Clayton Fountain was sustained by an amazing amount of hope, which he never relinquished, not even when he was almost crushed by disappointment.

If the word *miracle* is in any sense appropriate to this story, it is probably best reserved for me. Suspiciously, skeptically, and unwillingly, I slowly became one of the few people to accept as genuine Clayton's pilgrimage, one just as mystifying to him as it was to me. Our walk together became uncanny, especially when he came to the conviction that he was being called to the priesthood. I began to be haunted by a gnawing question, especially in strange dreams. "I'm nearing the end of a good life. Clayton is reaching his prime. If my taking Clayton's place in that cell could somehow free him to go to a seminary to study for the priesthood, would I be willing to do it?" After all, members of the Order of Mercedarians, founded in the thirteenth century, took a vow of willingness to offer themselves as hostages if necessary in order to rescue Christians who had been taken prisoner by the Moors. I knew that the question haunting my dreams was totally crazy, but it persisted. And out of my thinking and praying came a quiet conviction: I would do it.

From that point on, the meaning of my pilgrimage as Christian, monk, and priest became intertwined in an inexplicable way with Clayton's own spiritual quest. It was a saga that ended for me on July 11, 2005, in my monastic cemetery in the Ozark Mountains of Missouri . . .

But this is to jump far ahead in our story. The violent beginning with its irreparable downward spiral began on March 6, 1974. The scene opens with Clayton Fountain as an eighteen-year-old U.S. Marine stationed in Subic Bay, Republic of the Philippines.

CHAPTER TWO

Dancing with Death

———

The fateful event that would change the whole of Clayton's life occurred on the day when he murdered his Staff Sergeant at point-blank range with a 12-gauge shotgun. Although no one else really knew it, this was the crescendo of a tragedy that was a year in the making.

Clayton belonged to the 3rd Platoon of Hotel Company, 2nd Battalion, 4th Marines, distinguished as the "Raider Company." They were stationed at Camp Hansen in Okinawa, Japan. Shortly after arriving there, Clayton was placed on temporary duty assignment, and he left his unit to attend a parachute jump school run by the U.S. Army's 3rd Special Forces Group, where he was to earn his "jump wings" as a paratrooper.

Clayton's class was made up of personnel from different branches of the armed forces. In contrast to the other soldiers was a forty-year-old U.S. Air Force colonel who had barely met the entrance requirements. He was obviously out of shape, quite unaccustomed to the demanding physical exercise that would be required. Everyone expected him to "wash out" within weeks. But as the time passed, Clayton and the other Marines gained a respect for him, even beginning to admire the courage with which he persevered. As a result, they adopted him, almost as a mascot, giving him emotional and physical support — especially during the daily mandatory ten-mile runs.

In appreciation, the colonel used his contacts to arrange unofficial weekend transportation for his new friends. Clayton preferred to take the supply transport plane from Kadena Air Base on Okinawa to Subic Bay in the Philippines. He was particularly attracted to this place after hearing the colonel describe with suggestive detail his own erotic experiences there.

Clayton described these free weekends as making the most of "an exciting and exotic environment where women were eagerly and readily available, trying generally to raise hell and enjoy myself to the fullest in every possible way." His favorite routine was to bar-hop and carouse until martial law closed things down at 11:30 P.M. Afterwards he would "engage in a few lustful hours of what amounted to a sex marathon" with a bar girl in some hotel.

During one of these escapades, he met a woman using the bar name of "Sally," and at her invitation they spent the entire weekend together, mostly in bed. Although he wasn't clear about it at the time, when he later talked with me about the nature of this relationship, he concluded that "a large part of it was not love but pure lust." "Sally" was an attractive woman — five feet tall, slightly over a hundred pounds, with brown eyes, a smooth olive complexion, an abundantly attractive figure, and a personality that was "both vulnerable and pragmatic at the same time, with a rare straightforwardness and honesty." The magnetism between them made this the first of what became regular weekend adventures.

After completing his jump school training, Clayton returned to his unit. His entitlement to continue making parachute jumps on his liberty weekends provided a feasible explanation for his being "unavailable" when he was able to find a way to Subic Bay. After several months, his unit underwent a month of "Raider School." This consisted of advanced training in techniques of "hit-and-run" warfare to be conducted in enemy territory; nighttime parachute jumps; nighttime fighting techniques; silent nighttime movement; the use of plastic explosives; exten-

sive hand-to-hand combat; techniques in scaling up and rappel-
ling down obstacles; jungle escape survival; combat shooting;
guerrilla warfare; house-to-house fighting; security and riot-
control procedures; the detection and disarming of booby traps
as well as the construction and setting of them; jungle warfare;
sniper and counter-sniping techniques; sabotage; surveillance
and field interrogation of captured prisoners — and, above all,
"quick-kill" techniques of silently killing with hands, knife, and
garrote. Clayton was incredibly well-trained for the carnage that
he would soon leave in his path.

Because of a shortage of non-commissioned officers, Clayton was assigned as 3rd Platoon's 1st Squad Leader, which made
him "acting sergeant" even though he was only a Private First
Class. One day, everyone was given a three-day liberty pass, but
Clayton's Company Commander issued an order for an inspection the next morning. Failure to pass meant cancellation of the
leave and punishment with additional duty. As Clayton remembered that morning, recalling both feelings and graphic details,
the squad was sitting together on the floor, with Clayton super-
vising their cleaning of their rifles and gear — while they were listening to the radio, laughing, and telling ribald jokes.

Suddenly Staff Sergeant Wrin stepped through the door
without knocking and slammed a clipboard down on a man's
head, then began screaming obscenities at the top of his voice.
"As Staff Sergeant Wrin raised his clipboard to hit another of my
men," Clayton recalled, "I stepped in front of him and asked
him to step outside — to tell me why he was hitting my men and
shouting at them, since they had done nothing wrong. He
pushed me backwards, told me to 'f — k off,' and stated that he
didn't have to tell me anything because he outranked me.
Rather than argue with him, I ordered my squad to remain
seated while I went across the street to my platoon sergeant.
There I explained the problem, and asked for instructions on
what I should do. The platoon sergeant accompanied me back
to my quarters, where Staff Sergeant Wrin was still threatening
my squad and screaming obscenities. He was bluntly ordered
back to his own platoon area, and told to keep his hands off any-

one in 3rd Platoon, or he would face a general court-martial for assault."

This whole exchange lasted less than an hour, but it put into place the elements of a personal vendetta that would escalate relentlessly toward its violent ending — beginning Clayton's downward spiral into a maelstrom of violence, rage, vindictiveness, and murder. As Clayton saw it, Staff Sergeant Wrin felt insulted and embarrassed in front of the troops; he attempted to save face by retaliating, bringing formal charges against members of Clayton's squad. When Wrin commanded Clayton to sign the "charge sheets" without being told the nature of the charges, Clayton tore them up, dropped them into the trash can, and left with a barrage of curses following him. With this act, the plot was firmly in place, and from then on the dynamic would take on the shadow of inevitability.

The charges against the squad members were dismissed, and Staff Sergeant Wrin was reprimanded. But the matter didn't end there; it simply escalated. The Staff Sergeant, again insulted and embarrassed, allegedly charged Clayton with "insubordination." The dynamic between the two soldiers was feeding a full-fledged vendetta. As Clayton tells it, the harassment from Wrin became increasingly physical: he would beat Clayton severely "whenever I was isolated or caught alone, where there would be no witnesses present." Although Clayton became quite angry, he insisted that he didn't retaliate, knowing that to do so would provide immediate reasons for formal charges. Instead, Clayton brought charges against Wrin. Because of his rank, however, his superiors chose not to believe him. Feeling that he had no other option, Clayton began to fight back when Wrin attacked him. This was the only time that I ever heard Clayton admit that "although my fighting abilities and skills were very good, his were even better."

When three months of war games were scheduled, all troops were issued a four-day liberty pass. Clayton went to see "Sally," explaining that he would be unable to see her for quite a while. Although he wouldn't learn of it until three months later, when the war games ended, she was already four months' pregnant.

Because the war games were intended to simulate real combat, Wrin and Clayton used them as an opportunity to fight each other tooth and nail. In one encounter, Wrin backhanded Clayton across the mouth. Clayton called Wrin a "sadistic bastard" and spit a mouthful of blood in his face. Wrin retaliated by slamming a rifle butt into Clayton's chest, cracking three of his ribs. Although others observed this incident, it was judged "justifiable," being seen as "accidental."

After completing the war games, Clayton's battalion was assigned to serve aboard U.S. naval ships as a "combat-ready force," capable of deployment anywhere in the area of Southeastern Asia. When they docked in the Philippines, Clayton went immediately to see "Sally." Totally unaware of her pregnancy, he was shocked to see her with a hugely swollen stomach. While she insisted that the baby was his, he accused her of unfaithfulness. But he softened. "Without proof to the contrary," Clayton concluded, "I could only believe that she was telling the truth — and thus accepted the responsibility of fatherhood." The two of them would never be legally married, but they wore wedding bands and understood themselves as having a common-law marriage, even though neither the military nor United States law recognized it. Clayton later shared with me that if he hadn't gone to prison, he might have formally married her. Yet, he confessed, "in all honesty I know now that it would not have lasted. While we had a strong lust for one another, that lasts only for a short period, while true love needs to last and sustain a lifelong marriage."

Staff Sergeant Wrin continued to physically harass Clayton during the "float." Looking back on that time, Clayton admitted that he "was starting to become filled with hatred, rage, bitterness, and fear — feelings that over the months continued to grow and deepen, to an intensity that was frightening." Clayton believed that official forms of redress were closed, and he admitted to me how he felt about Wrin — something I never heard him say about any other person: "I was frightened of him, deeply." The situation in which he found himself he described as one of "isolation and betrayal."

When the Khmer Rouge had surrounded Phnom Penh, his

unit left port for the Gulf of Siam, and was put on "combat alert status." They were divided into six-man and twelve-man "killer teams" and flown by CH-46 helicopters into "landing zones." They infiltrated the Khmer Rouge lines, their purpose being to provide cover for the evacuation operation underway. Clayton later acknowledged that this assignment showed him just how much violence had become second nature to him. When he entered a conflict, his intent was to finish it — permanently.

In the middle of February 1974, Clayton held his son, then five months old, for the first time. Immersed as Clayton was in a totally violent environment, it was hard for him to embrace a new and contrary experience — yet he did: "It is impossible for me to describe the joy, love, and pride I felt as I held my son and watched him hold my right finger and suck on it. He was my son."

But such moments wouldn't last. On May 1, 1974, the dark crescendo approached. Clayton's unit was informed that a company inspection would be held the next morning, prior to their being given liberty passes. With such motivation, they spent the day and most of the night in preparation. When they finished, the platoon lieutenant ordered the platoon to fall out for a ten-mile run in physical training gear. When they completed the run, they returned to the ship, only to find that the inspection was still in progress. They were told to go to lunch dressed as they were, which was not normally allowed. The thirty Marines went into the mess hall as commanded, only to encounter Staff Sergeant Wrin. He ordered only Clayton to leave and "get properly dressed." Clayton obeyed and returned to his quarters, only to have the First Sergeant deny him entrance until the inspection was completed. Even though Clayton explained the situation, he was ordered back to the mess hall. When Staff Sergeant Wrin spotted him a second time, he didn't ask Clayton about the circumstances — he brought formal charges against him for insubordination.

On May 6, Clayton's commanding officer found him guilty of disobeying an order, but he agreed to drop the charge if the First Sergeant would verify that he had countermanded Staff Sergeant Wrin's order. When Clayton went in search of that officer, Staff

Sergeant Wrin saw him and asked where he was going. When Clayton told him, he exploded, as Clayton later explained: "He became enraged and proceeded to administer the worst beating I had received up until then. He told me he intended to kill me first, and then do the same to my infant son and 'the bitch' I lived with."

Clayton insisted that this was the threat that pushed him over the edge: "All the stored-up hatred, rage, bitterness, and fear exploded." He broke away from Wrin, and a short while later, "in a fear-fueled rage that is indescribable, I broke into the company armory and obtained a .45 caliber pistol and several magazines of ammunition." He left the ship and took a boat taxi to Grand Island, a resort for servicemen where he knew the sergeant would be attending a battalion party. Clayton disabled a guard, took his 12-gauge shotgun, found Staff Sergeant Wrin, and from a distance of three feet, shot him through the heart, killing him instantly.

Nearly delirious with anger and fear, Clayton saw that all avenues of escape were cut off at the docks. So he took five Marines hostage, resulting in a drawn-out standoff. Although one of the hostages was able to push Clayton off the pier, he was so agile that he climbed back on so quickly that no one was able to react. A military SWAT team was called in, and when they began pinpoint shooting, Clayton fled into an office building, taking two of the hostages with him.

A tense several hours passed; it was almost dark. Clayton shouted out the window that he would surrender if he could do so personally to his C.O. When he finally heard the boat taxi arriving, he went to the door with a hostage, only to be shot at with an M-14 rifle. The military police began to charge, but stopped when Clayton stepped out in the open with a shotgun aimed directly at them. Everyone froze; the scene pulsed with tension. Slowly Clayton lowered his weapon, placed it on the ground with his pistol, and surrendered. It was over. He was under arrest, escorted back to the ship under heavy guard.

Clayton faced numerous charges, the primary one being first-degree murder in violation of Article 118 of the Uniform

Code of Military Justice. Clayton was court-martialed, and on July 19, 1974, he was found guilty of all charges. He was sentenced to "confinement at hard labor for life," and given a dishonorable discharge. Although his military lawyers appealed the convictions, no one was surprised when they were summarily denied. While Clayton was in the brig, "Sally" was able to visit him. It was August when he held his son for the last time. He was never to see either of them again.

Clayton was transported to the U. S. Disciplinary Barracks at Fort Leavenworth, Kansas, where he began serving his sentence along with other life prisoners. The expectation was that this would be the end of the Clayton Fountain story. As it turned out, it was only the beginning.

CHAPTER THREE

Beyond Alcatraz

———————

For the first ten years of his incarceration, Clayton seemed fueled by a violent fire that fed on destruction and death. Looking back on this time, Clayton characterized himself as being "poisoned by fear, bitterness, hatred, and rage," which set in motion a relentless rampage of carnage.

At Leavenworth, it took Clayton only fourteen months to establish himself as "beyond control." The initial incident occurred when he threw cleaning fluid in an officer's eyes. But the determining act occurred on September 6, 1975, when he held a knife to the throat of a correctional officer. Using him as a hostage, Clayton gained access to both the prison's control room and the facility in which firearms were stored. There he took a shotgun and a pistol, and he fired three shots — one of which injured an officer when a bullet ricocheted off a wall. Clayton demanded to see the post commander, ostensibly to file a complaint. For this incident, he received an additional two-year sentence on December 11, 1975.

More incidents continued, and by January 1976 the U.S. Disciplinary Barracks had had enough of their role in the "Fountain story." They asked the federal prison system to accept custody of him — assuming, incorrectly, that the federal system would be better able to restrain him than they had been. The only neutral reference in his prison record was that he was employed as both morning and night cook, earning five hundred dollars a month.

In an act they no doubt came to regret, the Central Office of the Bureau of Prisons transferred Clayton on April 3, 1976, to their facility in Petersburg, Virginia. This time it took only one month for Clayton to make his mark: he earned reprimands for threatening another prisoner, being insolent to an officer, and exhibiting generally disruptive conduct and a defiant attitude. Clayton had become more than enough for this staff too, so they concluded that they weren't equipped to provide the security required to control him. On June 29, 1976, he was transferred to the higher security prison in Terre Haute, Indiana. To everyone's surprise, Clayton finally seemed to settle down, at least long enough for him to be placed in an honor housing unit. There he seemed to thrive on heavy work in a construction crew, receiving excellent reports. Apparently this hard labor was exhausting enough to slow the energy of his anger. But this was temporary: by year's end, he had assaulted an inmate and was found guilty of having a radio that had been altered against regulations.

Such behavior contributed to pushing Clayton further into his downward spiral. On June 4, 1977, he was sent as a "disciplinary transfer" to the very tough facility in Lewisburg, Pennsylvania. This time he set a near-record, taking only a month to be cited for insolence and disruptive conduct sufficient to land him in disciplinary segregation. Even this isolation didn't slow his aggressiveness; instead, it continued to mount — leading to a rapid recommendation that he be sent to the U.S. prison in Marion, Illinois, where almost all of the more than four hundred inmates were guilty of violent crimes. This was the institution specially built as the highest-security facility in the country, successor to the notorious Alcatraz after it was closed. At Marion, the operating philosophy was that if the most incorrigible prisoners were all put in one totally secure institution, the likelihood of violence would be lessened in the other prisons.

Clayton was sent to this "final destiny" with the full expectation that his violent history would come an end. Prison officials did their best to ensure this. From the very beginning they put

Clayton in a special unit that some called "the cellblock of last resort." It was reserved for the most hardened criminals.

Yet even there Clayton established a legendary record for violence that has little equal — and that still mystifies the authorities. He entered Marion on November 5, 1977, assigned to a nine-month residence in the Control Unit. Despite the severe restrictions of this unit, Clayton was charged with numerous disruptive incidents, from destroying government property to possessing explosive materials. Understandably, Clayton's stay in the Control Unit was extended.

For two years this isolation seemed sufficient to keep Clayton's hostility at a simmer. Then, on October 1, 1979, it erupted in full force. The official story is that Clayton and another prisoner stabbed Charles Stewart to death with a long metal object. Clayton's version is that Stewart was a homosexual predator who tried to rape his friend. Clayton insisted that it was Stewart who came at him with the knife, and after taking it away from him, Clayton stabbed Stewart over fifty times — threatening any officers who entered the cell "with the same." After stabbing his victim several more times, he surrendered. On April 24, 1980, Clayton received a ten-year sentence for manslaughter, with five additional years for possession of a weapon. Both sentences were to run consecutively to his previous life sentence.

After that incident, there were signs that Clayton's violence might be spent: he started to take an interest in improving himself, earning his GED certificate on November 29, 1979. But soon his record began to show his usual pattern: an escalating series of citations. Clayton was clearly at war with himself. On April 28, 1980, Clayton attempted an unheard-of escape. He and another prisoner somehow escaped from their cells and entered the plumbing access area; only after a search of the entire prison were they found in the utility pipe space, dressed in full riot gear — helmets, shields, gas masks, and batons. In the fight that ensued, a television set and several cans of paint were used as weapons. When the two men were captured, the authorities had seemingly run out of ideas about what to do. All they could think of was extending Clayton's stay in the Control Unit.

In 1981, Clayton again showed signs of improved behavior. Strange as it sounds, he decided to take a post–secondary education course in algebra. This time it took eleven months for the violence to erupt. On November 22, he and several other prisoners were accused of strangling to death Robert Marvin Chappelle during a recreation period. Another version of the story contends that Chappelle was asleep in his cell when they reached through the bars and killed him. Clayton denied taking any part in the killing. The prosecutors claimed that Chappelle was black and that his attackers were members of the Aryan Brotherhood, a group purported to be White supremacists. In conversations with me, Clayton consistently denied ever being a member of an Aryan group. Still, Clayton was convicted. On August 25, 1982, he and Thomas E. Silverstein were found guilty, and Clayton received yet another life sentence, to be served consecutively to his previous sentences.

This time the respite from violence was even shorter-lived. Only a month later, on September 27, 1982, Clayton and Thomas Silverstein were seen fighting with inmate Raymond L. Smith during recreation. Smith was stabbed sixty-seven times. Clayton argued that he fought in self-defense, after Smith sought revenge for the killing of his friend Chappelle. On May 24, 1984, Clayton received still another life sentence, this one likewise to run consecutively.

Nothing, apparently, could stop Clayton, and the killing spree intensified. On October 22, 1983, Clayton fatally stabbed a correctional officer, Robert L. Hoffman Sr., with a large knife, and wounded two other officers. The three were escorting Clayton back to his cell after recreation when somehow he managed to slip one of his hands free from his handcuffs and inexplicably gained access to a knife (perhaps handed to him through the bars by another prisoner); the deadly fight ensued. For this killing and the serious wounding of the other two men, Clayton received a fifty-year minimum and a 150-year maximum sentence, plus ten years for assault, and ten years for conveying a deadly weapon. In addition, he was ordered to pay restitution of over ninety thousand dollars to the victim's estate, and fifteen hundred dollars to the Department of Labor. Upon appeal, his sentence was changed to a life sentence, and the restitution amount was significantly reduced.

This carnage marked a record in the history of the U.S. Bureau of Prisons, forcing the authorities to admit that not even the highest security prison in the nation — perhaps the world — was able to control Clayton Fountain. In addition to his five killings, he had established a legendary record of misconduct, unique even within Marion history:

22 incidents of disruptive behavior, such as flooding his cell
14 incidents of destruction of government property
12 episodes of assault
11 episodes of possession of unauthorized material, such as handcuff keys
8 times of refusing orders
8 times of threatening another person
8 times of possession of a weapon
5 serious incidents of insolence
2 times of setting fires
2 times of refusing to follow safety regulations
1 incident of each of the following: conspiring to kill, threatening a staff member, possessing explosive materials, tampering with locking devices, adulterating food, making intoxicants, attempting escape, possessing drugs, and participating in a group demonstration

In addition, Clayton's record showed that "he has not maintained a significant work history," even though he was given numerous opportunities. Assignments included work in the recreation department, at UNICOR industries, in food service, in plumbing, electrical, and general construction, as well as assignments as education clerk, hospital orderly, and ward nurse. But from 1977 until the day of his death, Clayton was regarded as too dangerous to be assigned work that included others.

In near desperation, the highest prison authorities concluded on November 2, 1983, that they had no other option than to exercise the highly unusual action of individualized treatment. They built a special security unit in the U.S. Medical Center for Federal Prisoners in Springfield, Missouri, that cost forty thousand dollars. The full expectation was that this time Clayton Fountain had reached the end of the line — in whatever sense that might turn out to mean. That was exactly what happened — but in a way that no one could have imagined.

CHAPTER FOUR

Unto the Third and Fourth Generation

As the poet John Donne understood, no one is an island. But our interrelatedness is far more than external. No one comes untainted from the womb. We are what has been, knit into our genes and our memories. Living means making the best of it — for better or for worse. Each of us is a story, but there is always a story behind that story, with still others lurking behind these — stretching back, we are told, to a couple plucking forbidden fruit in an effort to "be like gods" (Gen. 3:5).

So it was that Clayton was never really alone in any of his cells, any place. Dark shadows entered with him, and they followed him wherever he was sent. But there was one in particular — one waiting for him even before he was born, both by presence and by absence.

It was Clayton's father, Raleigh, who loomed large in the Fountain family. He was imposing in both personality and vocation — which in his case were nearly identical. He was "career Army," as were several of Clayton's uncles, together destining Clayton to grow up as an "Army brat." "My earliest memories," Clayton told me, "were of things military." Clayton Anthony Fountain was born on September 12, 1955, at the U.S. Army Hospital in Fort Benning, Georgia. It took seven hours and twenty minutes for his mother, Ruth, to give birth to him. He was named after his father — whose full name was Clayton Raleigh Fountain — and he was expected to follow in his father's footsteps. And he did.

Clayton was the oldest of six children, having one brother and four sisters. All but one still live in Georgia, outside Savannah. The youngest sister may still be living in Dallas, Texas. The family moved with every new Army assignment that Raleigh received, usually every 1½ to 2 years. When his father served combat tours in Korea and Viet Nam and his mother was working, Clayton, as the oldest child in the family, became a surrogate for both parents when he was very young. He recalls maternal responsibilities for cooking, ironing, sewing, cleaning, and caring for his young siblings. It was the male/paternal role, however, for which his father had carefully trained him.

Clayton recalls that as far back as kindergarten and the first grade (when the family was in Germany), he was involved in numerous fights — purportedly in self-defense but especially in defense of his siblings. When his father was home, the family was ruled by an extension of military discipline, with Raleigh freely exercising corporal punishment for anything his quick temper interpreted as disobedience or "childishness."

Clayton remembers such an incident, which occurred when he was just four years old; its power would mark him. His father demonstrated how to use a knife by slitting a rabbit's throat, then rubbing the blood on Clayton's face and into his hair. When Clayton cried and vomited, Raleigh hit him and slapped him repeatedly, using his favorite refrain: "I'll teach you to be a man." Later, Clayton would lament, "I was never permitted to be a child — only a miniature macho man."

All that Clayton was permitted to want to be was a "warrior." His favorite game during playtime with other youngsters was one they called "war." When Clayton was only five, he received his first weapon. His father, uncles, and Army friends found great sport in teaching the young boy an amazing number of martial skills. As Clayton remembered it, the affirmation he could receive as a child came from practicing these skills "far better than was thought possible for someone so young." In such an environment, the only profession worth pursuing was soldiering. "One word characterized our family," Clayton told me. "What we did, what we thought, what we talked about — it was all about the military."

His mother remembers one triumphant letter she received from Clayton after he had become a Marine: "You can be proud of one thing. You have raised a man and a warrior!" Understandably, Clayton's reading had a specific focus, with his favorite comic books featuring Superman, Spider-Man, The Incredible Hulk, Wonder Woman, Conan the Barbarian, and G.I. Joe.

His father saw to it that "warrioring" was anything but theoretical, not only through the physical punishments he dealt out, but also in the considerable "friendly fighting" he did with Clayton. Clayton remembered their wrestling as becoming so real at times that "I had to fight back with all I had out of fear that I would be seriously injured." His mother chose silent submission instead of confrontation, later acknowledging tearfully the abuse that her non-action caused Clayton to experience. "I never reported Raleigh to the authorities because I was frightened of his anger. Besides, if they busted him, what would the rest of the family do?"

The family violence escalated in 1963 when they were living in Georgia. Clayton was around eight, and Raleigh was building a shed. Clayton wandered out with the intent of being with his father, but curiosity got the best of him — he wanted to see if a wire cutter could grasp an extension cord. The sparks that flew weren't only electrical. Raleigh smashed a board against Clayton's backside and then continued to express a rage so violent that it frightened the neighbors. When Ruth came home, she found her son in bed, a sheet concealing his body, which was covered with bruises, welts, and abrasions.

That, finally, was enough. Ruth left, and took the children with her. Although she later tried remarriage for a short time, her second divorce became final when Clayton was thirteen. Meanwhile, Clayton's father would be married and divorced several times. As his mother looks back on it now, she realizes that long before the first divorce, violence had made an indelible mark on

Clayton's personality, perhaps his character. He became increasingly aggressive, his violence triggered by a temper as quick as his father's. More and more frightened, Ruth sought psychological help for him, but this consisted mostly of medication, which provided only temporary relief.

Clayton joined the Marines at seventeen, lying about his age. His physique — 180 pounds, 5 feet, 9½ inches tall, with a build that indicated disciplined fitness — let him get away with it. He characterized himself as "hard-nosed, very tough, a 'by-the-book' individual who saw things as either black or white, right or wrong, with no shades of gray. I followed orders precisely and expected others to do the same, and if they did not, I would drop on them like a ton of bricks — no give, no excuses, no compromises. I knew my military skills, and I demanded that everyone else be as good — or better." This was the dynamic that seemed destined to rule his future.

Clayton's regard for his mother seems to have been mostly positive, yet he was uneasy about the gentle virtues, seeing them as "unmanly." Once he mentioned that his mother used drugs and that during one of the times she was "using," she shot him in the leg with a .22 pistol. There were hints of other abuse. Yet there was only one incident, which happened when he was older, that caused a significant falling out between them. Clayton referred to it more than once. To help pay for his education while in prison, Clayton asked his mother to sell the cherished rifle that his father had given him. She put him off repeatedly, until his persistence forced her to confess: she had already sold it a while ago, and hadn't told him. This betrayal, as he called it, plus his disapproval of the man his mother was dating at the time, caused a rift between them. Eventually, however, mother and son were reconciled. From then on, Clayton would frequently express concern over how hard his mother had to work, how little money she had, and how helpless he felt concerning her situation.

Clayton maintained good relations with his married sisters, but some of them never told their children about their uncle's incarceration or explained why he never visited. Another sister, mentally disabled, was supported by the state. Clayton was especially close to a cousin with whom he had grown up. His one brother was, in a sad way, like him: he was — and may still be — in jail somewhere on the East Coast.

Clayton almost never talked about his father unless I asked about him. Clearly there was a love-hate relationship between them, which caused a rupture that would be reconciled — ironically, as we shall see — only when both of them were dead. I've often wondered to what degree the killing of Staff Sergeant Wrin was in reality an unconscious vengeance that Clayton wreaked upon his father.

Clayton's psychological health is certainly an issue aching to be raised. To the best of my knowledge, he was given only three psychological tests. Nowhere in his records, or in conversations with prison personnel, was his sanity ever questioned.

The results of the "Firo-B Relationship Test" indicated that while Clayton was very friendly and outgoing, he preferred little social interaction. He was selective in choosing close friends, but he was comfortable with them, in both showing and receiving warmth. He didn't expect an excessive amount of attention or closeness from other people, nor did he apparently need it. The test results also indicated that Clayton had a healthy balance between a need for control and an acceptance of direction. However, he preferred to use his own leadership skills, and he became bored and frustrated where and when these were denied. He showed himself to be confident, approaching situations realistically, rarely overestimating or underestimating his ability. He set high goals, was comfortable with making decisions and taking responsibility for them, and had no particular need to control others. He had a good self-concept, and thus he was able, more easily than most people, to accept someone who was not friendly toward him.

The "Culture Free Self-Esteem Inventory" gave these results:

Overall perception of worth: high
Quality of relationship with peers: high
Intimate perceptions of self-worth: very high
Total: very high

The Myers-Briggs Personality Inventory showed Clayton's personality type to be "INFJ" — "introvert," "intuitive," "feeling," and "judging." I found this test prophetic of the Clayton who would emerge over time. People with this personality type succeed through perseverance, originality, and the desire to do what's necessary, thereby putting forth their best efforts. They are quietly forceful, conscientious, concerned for others, and thus they are respected for their firm principles and clear convictions in serving the common good. They relate to the outside world with their feelings; internally they are guided by intuition.

Introverts favor a quiet environment in order to concentrate, and they tend to think before they act. They prefer to communicate through writing, and they learn best through reading. Intuitives thrive on new challenges and possibilities, work in bursts of energy, dislike repetition, are powered by enthusiasm, and ask why things are as they are.

Feeling types are good at seeing the impact of their choices on others. They like harmony, tend to be sympathetic, and enjoy pleasing people. Judging types like to plan ahead, get things settled and finished, and work step-by-step to meet their goals on time. These types tend to be drawn toward vocations as clergy, psychiatrists, social workers, writers, teachers, and artists.

All of these factors converged in creating the person who on April 1, 1985, was brought in shackles by the heaviest security force possible to his new "home" — a tailor-made place of guaranteed isolation at the Federal Medical Center in Springfield, Missouri. The prison authorities were certain that Fountain's future would finally be totally uneventful. They were wrong. Clayton's life would be eventful — but in a new, nonviolent way.

One of the authorities who was waiting for him made it clear that they knew exactly who they had been bequeathed: "We knew without question that he was a ruthless murderer who needed neither reason nor provocation for his deadly actions, about which he had no sense of guilt." He came to the Federal Medical

Center as a total enigma — a perfectly sane man who acted insanely, a person of exceptional intellect who acted without thought, a person of principles who destroyed without excuse, justification, or mitigating circumstances. When he arrived, the key to his cell was, for all intents and purposes, thrown away.

Looking back on the first time I visited him in his original isolation cell, I recall that it was on the second floor east in the Special Housing Unit. It was at the end of a long hall of solitary confinement cells, some of which had been emptied to guarantee Clayton's total isolation. The cell had been redone, with a door opening into a smaller room in which he could exercise. I couldn't see into the cell, but photographs I acquired later indicate a very narrow cell with a barred, opaque window on the far wall, a combined sink-toilet unit, a small television, a concrete-anchored bed, and a barred window looking out to the tiled hallway, beside which was a telephone for communicating with the occupant. A light high in the ceiling was permanently lit, with a 24-hour audio and visual security surveillance system, and a two-way speaker.

The intent was to keep Clayton totally cut off from all interaction with other prisoners. His only human contact was to be restricted to assigned staff or the warden. Despite such designs, however, it's not surprising that Clayton found a way to communicate with other prisoners in solitary confinement through the air ducts, as well as by tapping in code on the water pipes.

Only rarely during his twenty-one years in solitary confinement was Clayton taken from his cell. These occasions involved semi-annual regional review hearings, held near his cell, and rare medical or dental attention. On such occasions, Clayton was restrained with two pairs of handcuffs securing his hands behind him, an electric belly belt (constructed so that any abrupt movement would render him temporarily senseless), and two pairs of leg shackles; he was escorted by a supervisory lieutenant and from three to five regular guards. Once he was taken to the hospital for X-rays of his back. He was escorted early in the morning before there was any traffic. Three official vehicles were involved, the first and the third filled with armed guards. Clayton was in the second vehicle with guards; he was fully shackled and wearing the electric belt. Another time, a doctor needed to enter his cell. For this visit, Clayton's hands and feet were handcuffed to braces embedded in his concrete bed.

As a monastic hermit, I've been formed to live creatively in solitude — and to thrive on it. In that sense, Clayton's living situation and mine weren't that different — but the enormous difference was rooted in the fact that Clayton never chose such isolation. An experience I had in the late 1960s helped to sensitize me to this major difference. At that time I was a seminary professor, and I preferred to use a fairly radical action-reflection type of learning technique. Always in search of interesting learning "exposures" for my students, I asked permission to experience for myself a three-day incarceration in Leavenworth Federal Penitentiary. Since it was important that the experience be as authentic as possible, the arrangement was that after I was brought to the prison gate, no one with whom I would relate would know anything about me, other than that I must be a transfer from another institution.

Within several minutes of my entrance, I began feeling strange emotionally, a feeling triggered simply by the way I was being escorted. This feeling increased when a guard explored my "personal extremity" for contraband with his gloved fingers. And that was just the beginning. Next I was quickly stripped of my clothes and observed intently as I showered in an open room. I spent much of my time at the prison in the "hole" — the complete isolation reserved for problem prisoners. There was nothing to do, nothing even to stare at in my cell — only a barred, opaque window, a toilet, a sink, an anchored, steel-spring bed, and one blanket (no pillow). Overhead, a stark, solitary light was like a non-blinking eye that watched me day and night, forbidding me to try to sleep. Most haunting was a tiny slot in the steel door. At unpredictable times, day and night, it would slide open, and an eye would stare in at me — just stare.

Each time the eye appeared, my resentment increased. But that's putting it too mildly. I felt a mounting hostility. Once I spit in its direction. I was tempted to try to inform prison officials —

even though they'd never believe me — that this wasn't for real. But it was. They didn't know the circumstances. It was becoming "me" versus "them." I was in isolation for only three days, but even during that short time, an incipient anger began rising in me, as if necessary for preserving any personal integrity in the midst of being nothing but a number. Clayton would experience this for twenty-one years.

I still remember how I felt when "they" finally came to release me. I refused to speak to or even look at the guard — or any other authority figure — as I was escorted to the front door, and freedom. I never completely lost the feeling evoked by that experience. Maybe — just maybe — I got a hint of the dynamic enfolding the person I came to know as the "old" Clayton. In turn, it gave me a hint of how special the gentleness of the "new" Clayton would be.

Clayton's cell, worse still than mine, was where he began what he came to call his five-year "trial by fire." Much of the time he was blind to what only later he was able to identify as "the process by which God relentlessly purged me of my inner poisons — my hatred, rage, bias, bitterness, revenge, vengeance, violence — all those things that had been controlling me." No one will ever know — at least with any certainty — what actually happened in that cell during this time. Clayton later described it to Father Robert, a hermit from our Trappist monastery who was to become his first spiritual director. "The isolation became so horrendous that I knew beyond a shadow of a doubt that if ever I were to walk out of this hole as a free man, something radical had to change." Still later, he gave me a more succinct version: "If I ever hoped to get out, I had to change."

I'm convinced that Clayton's passion for freedom was what first motivated him. Ironically, he found the initial strength for his change in the same disciplined military determination to gain control that had lured him down the wrong path. This time it became focused on positive self-discipline. Symbolically, on the day he decided to change, he stopped smoking — cold turkey. However we understand what happened to Clayton inside, the indisputable fact is that he stopped engaging in violence too

— cold turkey. Beginning January 16, 1986, three years after first occupying the cell, Clayton would never again be cited for misconduct of any kind. From that date onward, his official record reads, under the category of adjustment, "good," and under rapport with staff, "commendable." In time, even the warden was forced, grudgingly, to acknowledge that outwardly Clayton's turnaround was "remarkable."

But would it last? Was it real? Five years after this turnaround, the conclusion of the warden's report remained dismal: "Clayton Fountain must still be considered an extreme security risk based on his serious history of violence."

I am convinced that Clayton's initial change was based on a tenacious willpower, an obstinate self-determination, an emotional "white-knuckling." I liken it to my own desperate — but successful — effort to stop smoking, ironically provoked by deep anger over my awareness that I was unable to stop. While such resoluteness can be effective in the short run, perseverance in the long run depends on going beyond changed behavior — to becoming a changed person. The will that wills the good can just as quickly will the evil, given changed circumstances of self-interest. This would be the issue shadowing Clayton's entire pilgrimage from then on, until his death — and beyond.

Years later, when Father Robert and I discussed this period of Clayton's life, we agreed that while his change of behavior was indeed amazing, without something more, neither of us would have trusted it in the long run.

Something more did happen — something that would lead him toward the spirituality of a Trappist monk. In decided contrast, Thomas E. Silverstein, Clayton's co-conspirator in two of the Marion murders, was incarcerated in Leavenworth, and there he remains. The last report I heard was that he has become "a caged animal."

CHAPTER FIVE

Exposé and Its Reversal

On December 17, 1989, an amazing and extensive "Special Report" was published in the daily Springfield *News-Leader*. It was an exposé of Clayton Fountain, its main article entitled "The Most Dangerous Man." It was subtitled "Med Center's Maze Holds Cold Killer." The featured photograph was one of Clayton taken immediately after he had killed a prisoner in 1982, showing blood running from a puncture wound in his upper right chest, where he had been stabbed during the fight. Another article was entitled "Abusive Army Father at Root of Would-be Warrior's Rages." Still another detailed the gory side of Clayton's Marion killings, while still another was a bitter interview with a former guard who had survived one of Clayton's stabbings.

These articles converged forcefully to create an image of Clayton Fountain as "a man so deadly that he cannot be trusted even to touch another human being" — totally unrepentant, plagued by inner demons, a "flinty-eyed killer." The warden at that time, C. A. Turner, spoke for most: "Clayton is a cold, calculating killer. Some people kill in a fit of passion, or for some other reason. I doubt there is anybody else who has committed as many calculated murders as he has." While Turner admitted, skeptically, that for six years Clayton had demonstrated amazing "exemplary behavior," U.S. attorney Fredrick Hess drew the bottom line for himself and for most others: "I see no value in the preservation of his life."

I've tried to discern what the motivation might have been for these articles, since the reporter, Ron Davis, had the highly unusual cooperation of the prison authorities, to the highest level. Not only was he given the unprecedented right to conduct two interviews with Clayton outside his cell; he also was permitted to give Clayton a 76-question survey and have access to his military and court records. In addition, he gained access to a number of Clayton's personal letters to his family. This material was interlaced with interviews of over forty people in six states and the District of Columbia.

The conclusion I've drawn is that the authorities expected the articles to encourage public support for federal death-penalty legislation, at least for any person found guilty of killing prison personnel. In fact, in testimony before a Senate subcommittee considering the death penalty, Bureau of Prisons Director Norman Carlson used Clayton as a supreme example of why such legislation should be enacted. Perhaps it was hoped that the articles would help justify more stringent control methods in the federal prison system. Whatever lay behind them, it was these articles, written with a reporter's eye for the sensational, that infuriated Clayton's family. Yet they remain the only extensive public reporting of the "Fountain legend."

Although they were probably intended to be a call for capital punishment, the irony is that they ended up effecting a transformation in Clayton that made a powerful case for just the opposite. It happened this way. One day after the newspaper stories appeared, a woman I'll call Beth wrote a five-page letter to the Medical Center addressed to "Most Dangerous Prisoner Clayton Fountain." Almost no one but Clayton has read that letter, but recently I found a copy. With the same direct assertiveness that I later discovered to be her nature, Beth began this way: "Well, they can lock you in a special cell, but they can't keep you from encountering God — only you can do that. Because I know from personal experience that God is still in the business of miracles,

I feel I must write to you." What followed was her vulnerable confession, which was amazing because she risked sharing it with a person she had never met — and never would. She claimed that she had been a "wild, raving atheist" for half her life. She detailed her life of cursing, drinking, drugs, endless affairs, and dabbling in the occult, complete with verbally and emotionally abusing two husbands into divorces.

A year ago, she continued, she met a married man in a bar, and they bedded down for the night. To her surprise, she found herself falling in love for the first time. Previously she denied "having a heart," describing it as "only a pimple on my left kidney." Whatever it was, it ached in a way she had never known before. "One night, in desperation, 'Beth' the atheist got down on her 44-year-old knees and cried out, 'Dear God, what am I going to do about this mess in my life?'" The next morning as she was crying, she heard a loud voice inside her head screaming "STOP FORNICATING!!!" In one sense her experience paralleled Clayton's up to this point — but with one major difference. As she put it, "I knew that it was God speaking, and my whole life was changed."

Beth's conversion occurred in July 1986. Her behavior over the next three years gave credence to her conviction that "in that one instant, God set me free from bondage to unbelief, to alcohol, to an immoral lifestyle, and to filthy language." She separated this experience from any church, any preaching, because it happened privately, in the solitude of her own bedroom cell, as it were. It was "unexpected, breathtaking, and totally undeserved." The classic word for this would be "grace."

Beth said that God was "in control," that "nothing that happens is an accident," that "the unseen world of the Spirit is the real world," and that "God does things in his own way, for his own reasons, and according to his own timetable." (Later I would hear Clayton use these same words quite often.) "God's ways are not our ways," she continued, and so with a powerful certainty she affirmed as fact that Clayton A. Fountain was no mistake, that God had a plan for his life, and that it was God's will that no person should be lost, least of all Clayton. "God is calling, and all you need to do is listen to your heart, and then to ask and keep on asking; seek and keep on seeking; knock and keep on knocking." The door will be opened, and forgiveness will be offered — sufficient to "wash away your scarlet past, and place you, clean and new, in today — free of your chains."

Beth then became personal again, telling Clayton that the only employment she had was caring for an elderly lady, and thus she had very little money. Yet she would be willing to save enough money to buy him a Bible if he didn't have one; she preferred the New International Version. She ended by offering a prayer for Clayton, "for the soul of this precious one who needs you desperately . . . , that he might be brought back from the dead, as you have done with me. Amen." Her postscript was cryptic: "Many people want you dead, but God has preserved your life. Why?"

I never met Beth, nor have I been able to find her. But a person who has met her described her as a woman of medium height with a heavy build, brown hair, and an ordinary face, a woman "who had lived a lot and looked it." She was intelligent and sensitive. She was in no way shy, yet although she was opinionated, she could listen. Above all, she was passionate about whatever was going on.

I've acquired a copy of Clayton's response, dated December 22, apparently written the very day he received Beth's letter. Interestingly, her meticulous handwriting — perfectly straight, controlled printing — paralleled Clayton's meticulously written and perfectly straight, controlled script. His letter was polite, expressing appreciation for her "encouragement" and the promise of her prayers. Yet there is no evidence that he really heard her witness. Instead, he insisted that for the past six years he had been the one who had been working to improve himself, knowing full well the "long road ahead of me."

He explained to her that prisoners weren't allowed to receive books from private sources, but said that that didn't matter because the chaplain's office had supplied him with a Bible. He told Beth about working on a bachelor's degree through correspondence courses, majoring in pre-law/business with a hope of someday attending law school. He said he saw his education as being the central vehicle for his "improvement and changes for the better." Success, he concluded, depended on "whether I work hard enough."

Clearly, Clayton didn't yet have a clue about what Beth was telling him. Working hard toward self-improvement is completely different from totally surrendering one's powerlessness to the undeserved grace of God. Their two pilgrimages toward change were diametrically opposed. Yet through their ongoing exchange of letters, this difference gradually started to illumine Clayton's life, beginning a slow transformation that was to continue until his untimely death. A Catholic deacon who later worked with Clayton put it this way: "It was Beth's experience of being down and out that finally brought him the hope that he really needed."

None of the letters between the two of them remain, so I'm dependent on Clayton's quoting from them in conversations we had and letters he wrote to me. As he told me, "She was the one who opened my heart to true love for the first time. And therein came the breakthrough — that God had not only always loved me, but still did and was waiting to welcome me into his arms. All I needed to do was accept his love. It was with a profound sense of shock, wonder, and awe that I finally came to understand that God loved even me — a man with the life-blood of five people on his hands and conscience. God was willing to meet me right where I was."

As Clayton later wrote, the primary event in his life up to that point occurred one night in his cell during February 1990. "I confessed, repented, asked forgiveness, and invited and accepted Jesus into my heart and life as Lord and Savior." With this transition, Clayton's search for direction took its spiritual turn.

I wish we could know more about the increasingly intense letters between Beth and Clayton, which formed a dynamic all their own. Although the two of them were never to meet, they began sharing feelings. In fairly rapid progression, the word *love* appeared — and then expressions of it. During this same time, Beth began exploring Catholicism as the direction in which the

Spirit might be leading her. She entered an RCIA ("Rite of Christian Initiation of Adults") explorers' class at St. Agnes Catholic Church in Springfield, intending, if she persevered, to receive baptism. Clayton agreed to undergo a parallel exploration under the supervision of the Catholic prison chaplain. Beth sought and was granted annulments of her two marriages — so that within about three months of the first letter, Beth and Clayton had discussed the possibility of marriage, explored it, and then mutually agreed to it.

Beth asked Clayton to do something that would be very difficult for him. He agreed, and at three P.M. on July 22, 1990, he painfully began a six-page, handwritten confession of his killing of Staff Sergeant Douglas Wrin. The most notable feature of this description was that never once did Clayton attempt to justify his actions. This was an important milestone. From then on, he was able to be vulnerable with the few people who cared about him. During the years of our relationship, Clayton sometimes asked to correspond with a friend of mine who sounded interesting. In each case, he sent with his letter a copy of this confession, wanting the person to know what kind of person he had been, so that they could decide "with full knowledge" if they wished to respond.

But two deep disappointments lay ahead for Clayton — disappointments that would test the authenticity of his small beginnings in his spiritual quest. The first occurred when it was about time to make a decision concerning baptism. Beth concluded that she was no longer "comfortable" in continuing, explaining that while she intended to "follow Christ," she could not stomach the "crap" that joining the Catholic Church would involve.

To the best of my knowledge, she was never baptized. Yet Clayton remained convinced that this was the direction that God desired for him. As a result, there occurred what was perhaps one of the most bizarre administerings of the sacrament in Catholic Church history. On Easter, April 19, 1992, Clayton was baptized and confirmed into the Roman Catholic Church. On that day, perhaps for the first time since he had arrived at the prison, the double steel door creaked open, and guards dared to enter the dank, tomb-like cell. Clayton was handcuffed and fitted with shackles, and when it was considered "safe," Father Nelson Garcia entered. Then, with a lieutenant and six officers as witnesses, in the presence of all the angels and saints, as the liturgy testifies, Clayton A. Fountain descended through water into the tomb of Christ's death, three times for the three days in the tomb, and rose with Christ into the forgiven life of a new creature. So cleansed, he received for the first time the body of Christ broken for him, promising to break away the encrusted death of his old life, and he raised "the cup of eternal salvation" as a toast to the God of his new beginnings.

After this ceremony, the cell doors clanged shut, and once again Clayton was back in the lonely, endless days of total solitude. Yet, looking back on it, he found this event to be the beginning of a dynamic by which this tiny place in space and time would be sanctified as "no longer my burial place but an emptied tomb, for I had become a prisoner for Christ."

The second testing of Clayton's professed conversion began when the warden refused Beth and Clayton's request to be married — in fact, refused to allow them even to meet. In one of her last letters to Father Robert (a relationship I will describe later), Beth shared her conclusion that since marriage wasn't possible, and since she couldn't wait for a less-than-certain parole, it seemed best "to drop completely out of Clayton's life." In a written reflection at a later point, she put it this way: "For several months now I have been involved in the process of disentangling my life from Clayton's, and thereby reducing his dependence on me."

She completed the separation during August of 1992. In a note she wrote to a friend, she described the "divorce" more theologically: "I gave Clayton back to God. The image God gave me was of a man training for his private pilot's license: study first, then fly with an instructor pilot. Then the day comes when it is time to solo. There are things God has in mind for Clayton to do, and these I cannot help him with."

Several months later, she became less cerebral about the

separation: "It was fully as difficult to release Clayton as it was to become his friend at the beginning. Persecution has been intense for me from my family and friends, and even from other Christians, because of my intimate and personal involvement with Clayton." With this understanding, she wrote to Father Robert that she was handing Clayton over to his care, for "you can help him better now than I can." With that, she disappeared from all of our lives.

To this day, I find remarkable Clayton's response to Beth's "abandonment" of him. Now it was over; the commitment was broken. She had walked away. These were hard months for Clayton — terribly hard. He was hurt, and he wrestled with the temptation of bitterness. Yet his response was totally out of character for the angry, out-of-control Clayton of Marion. There was no trace of the behavior that everyone had come to expect of him. Instead of anger and rage, he showed deep sadness and disappointment. Never once — then or ever — did he say anything negative about Beth, insisting instead that this relationship was the first time in his life that he had ever known love. He always spoke of her with fond respect and deep thankfulness. Several different times he described the experience in the same way: "A fine Christian lady entered my life, looked beyond what I had done to what I could be, and once I knew such love, what followed was simply living it out."

There's more to this episode. Fourteen years later, a friend of mine asked if she might write a letter of support to Clayton, and to promise to pray for him. I was oblivious to the fact that her name, too, was Beth. During my next visit to the prison, Clayton showed me the letter she had written, simply signing it "Beth." For the week since he had received it, he had fully believed that he was hearing again from the "other" Beth, that she was reaching out to him after all those years. Clayton's response was telling. Although he felt bewildered, he was inclined not to respond, choosing instead to be thankful for what had happened and "needing nothing more." When I explained the situation of "the two Beths," he showed no anger, not even disappointment. If anything, he seemed slightly relieved.

The last time that anyone I have come across saw "the first Beth," it was in connection with a graduate program in Pastoral Studies and Education sponsored by Loyola University. Beth was one of nine members of a learning group that met in Springfield. In 1993, with the completion of the third course, one concerned with the New Testament, Beth left the group, indicating that while she was interested in Scripture, Catholic morality and "church stuff" weren't for her. Before she left, however, she shared with the group a rough draft of a required paper entitled "How I Understand My Faith Experience and Ministry through Jesus." Interestingly, she used her "prolific correspondence with Clayton" as her defining faith experience — not her own conversion experience. She shared as critical that Clayton had begun to wrestle with a concern that was to become existential for him later on, when he would petition the warden for release into the general prison population. For him, living as a faithful Christian might well mean sacrificing his life rather than retaliating when threatened by another prisoner. Beth concluded her sharing with her pastoral group by saying that after Clayton's baptism, God had said to her, "You can relax now, Beth. The church will take it from here."

The part of this story that most perplexes me is Beth and Clayton's proposed marriage. So when I came to know a woman who married a prisoner on death row, I timidly asked if she could shed any light on the dynamics between Clayton and Beth. She was a reporter, and she interviewed this prisoner several times for a story — in a way, she insisted, that was strictly professional. When she realized that she had personal feelings for this man, she investigated his past, interviewed his defendants, and read the case records. In the process, she became convinced that he was innocent of the charge of murder, and began helping him with his case. She acknowledged forthrightly that "I would most likely have felt differently about him had there been evidence that he had taken another's life." But, she ventured, "We do not choose the people with whom we fall in love. In our case, and maybe in Clayton's case, God did the choosing, even though my prisoner friend was an atheist at the time. Neither of us wanted a relationship, and certainly neither of us planned to care about the other."

She acknowledged the stereotype of women who become involved in prison relationships — that they are "emotionally needy, abused, insecure, and intellectually deficient." She understood clearly that only 5 percent of prison marriages last — because it takes a very strong, independent, resilient person to persevere. The price is being "viewed as an abhorrent oddity, a retarded child, shunned by friends and family alike. You face long, lonely nights, and about even the good times of prison visits, no one wants to hear." In the end, she concluded, "it's a matter of believing in our hearts that we are better people for relating to each other than we would be without each other." I've concluded that this is about as close to understanding this matter as I'm likely to get.

At this point I need to pick up an important thread of this story, one that began several years before the Clayton-Beth correspondence. Beth had written to my monastery, Assumption Abbey, near Ava, Missouri, which is an hour and a half from Springfield. She asked the abbot for someone with whom she as "a seeker" could correspond. When none of the other monks were interested in doing so, Father Robert reluctantly entered the story by agreeing to write to her. He began writing once a month, and did so over a period of several years. He characterized Beth's letters as a sharing of what she did, what she experienced, and how she felt about life — not involving spiritual direction in the usual sense. Actually, he sometimes wondered if what she really wanted was simply a friendly pen pal.

Once she came to the monastery with her mother to meet Father Robert personally. Then in a letter she told him that she was angry with him because, as she put it, "you refuse to share your feelings with me." This made him uneasy about her real motives. She would stop writing periodically, only to begin again — it was off and on. When she began writing to Clayton, her correspondence with Father Robert became minimal, and finally stopped.

She did write one further letter to him, in which she shared Clayton's need for financial aid in continuing his education and expressed her hope that the monastery could help. After that, Father Robert wrote to Clayton and eventually made a commitment to write to him monthly. Within several months, Clayton asked for permission to call him monthly for half an hour. The time chosen was eleven A.M. on the first Saturday of each month. At first, Clayton's letters indicated little more than an interest in having a pen pal. Increasingly, however, they became an outlet for expressing his feelings about life. Beth had sent Father Robert the newspaper articles about Clayton, so from the beginning he knew something about Clayton's background. I asked his motive for originally writing to Clayton. "It was my Christian duty," he told me. He was "obeying the scriptural injunction to minister to those in prison."

Clayton's early letters were written in longhand, in a script as meticulously tight and controlled as his military upbringing. When the warden permitted Clayton to do some part-time work as a clerk/typist, he was provided with a used typewriter, which was replaced when it broke. Then, when Clayton was doing his college work by correspondence (which I will describe later), one of his teachers had a brother who lived in Springfield who was willing to give Clayton an antiquated Brother Word Processor (5500DS). This he quickly mastered. Later, when it broke too, the prison authorities provided Clayton with a used Dell System OptiPlex GX-110 computer equipped for Windows 2000, with a Hewlett-Packard DeskJet 840C printer — but without Internet access.

Early in their conversations, Father Robert planted a seed in Clayton that would bear fruit later. He drew a parallel between Clayton's prison cell and his own hermitage. While Father Robert had chosen his isolation, he suggested that a change of perspective on Clayton's part could transform his imposed solitude into a spiritual place of choice. The difference, he suggested, depended on whether, when one looked out between the prison bars, one saw mud or saw stars. "Keep your eyes on what uplifts," Father Robert instructed. Gradually their letters shared an awareness of God's presence in Clayton's isolation, and it was Clayton's conviction that he was not really alone that gave him hope for the future, no matter how vague.

Here we might pause for a moment to look for trail markers in this story that might hint that the changes in Clayton were authentic. I recall a letter that Father Robert wrote to a moral theologian in San Francisco, asking a question that had been haunting Clayton. It was "whether a prisoner is obliged to try to prevent unjust acts on a fellow convict, even if his interference would almost certainly lead to a life-death struggle." On July 27, 1990, the response came — that the Christian is not under a strict obligation to defend the weak, but that charity obliges one to try, if no danger to the self is involved. Otherwise, it would be an act of "heroic charity."

What is important is not so much the answer itself but how the question reflects the beginning of Clayton's reliving his past from the "what-if" perspective of a Christian. Originally his thinking about his early acts was done in terms of his "rights." Here we can observe a shift in perspective, for now his ruminations became a way of exploring his Christian "duty."

Initially Clayton justified each one of his killings in terms of his "rights," stressing his right to self-defense. His military training had established a them-or-me syndrome that had become a way of life. "I killed to prevent myself from being killed," he had said. No matter how it starts, "the right of defense" makes sure that you are the one who finishes it. Any disagreement, almost by definition, thereby has the potential for escalating into a deadly dynamic.

Actually, Clayton never knew civilian life. The transition from the Marines to prison simply extended his operative war zone. By the time I came to know him, he was willing to answer any questions I asked. Not once did I sense that he needed to defend his behavior anymore. He simply confessed as fact that he had been wrong — not only in what he did but in who he was. "My behavior was a true expression of who I really was then, but, God willing, I no longer am."

Another milestone was Father Robert's transition from skepticism to trust in Clayton's spiritual authenticity. While in Marion, Clayton sued the government, alleging that the guards had treated him violently. He won the suit and was awarded a settlement of a thousand dollars. On July 20, 1992, Clayton wrote this letter to the widow of the officer that he had killed:

Dear Mrs. Hoffman,

I am forwarding this letter to you in care of the U.S. Attorney's Office, in the hope that you will eventually receive it, although I realize that I am, perhaps, the last person you want — or ever expected — to ever hear from. Writing you this letter is one of the hardest tasks I have ever had to do, owing to a sense of fear I have never before experienced, but it is something God has called me to do — so it must be done, even if you do not believe me.

My purposes for writing you are: (1) To send you the enclosed $800.00 as a partial payment of the $2,557.45 restitution debt I owe to the estate of Robert Hoffman, Sr.; and (2) To ask you to forgive me for the death of your husband on 22 October 1983 — although I realize that you may not be able, or willing, to do so.

Beginning in December, 1989, God called me — through the love of a wonderful Christian lady — and in March 1990, I accepted Jesus Christ into my life as my Lord and Savior, and became a Christian. Shortly after [I became] a Christian, God began a process of leading me to the Christian "home" he had for me, which much to my surprise turned out to be the Catholic Church. On 19 April 1992, Easter Sunday, I was officially baptized and confirmed into the Catholic Church.

You are probably wondering what all this has to do with my purposes for writing you. The answer lies in Matthew 5:23-24, which says: "Therefore, if you are offering your gift at the altar and there remember that your brother has something against you, leave your gift there in front of the altar. First go and be reconciled to your brother, then come and offer your gift." Although I did not immediately understand why this had such an impact upon me when I read it, I contemplated and prayed about it. God began revealing the path I was being called to follow — which included sending you the enclosed $800.00 and asking for your forgiveness.

At first, I resisted God's calling because the $800.00 is all the money I have to my name, and I desperately need it. I also resisted because writing this letter caused an extreme sense of fear that I have never before experienced. The more I resisted, however, the more God convicted me of what I was being called to do — and that was/is to obey and rely solely upon Him in all things.

Although I am not "legally" required to make restitution until — or unless — I am released from prison, God has very clearly called me to send you all I have as a partial restitution payment. While I cannot yet complete paying the remaining restitution I owe your family, God requires me to do what I can, and with God's help I will pay it as I can.

Money cannot begin to make up for your loss, but it is all I can do to help demonstrate the regret and sorrow I feel for having been the person responsible for the death of your husband. Yet I am asking your forgiveness for the loss, pain, and grief you have had to endure.

Please forgive me, Mrs. Hoffman, and accept my heartfelt apologies. And if you can find it in your heart to pray for me, I would count that a rich blessing. Please know that you will always be remembered in my daily prayers. And I will, by God's grace, continue to demonstrate my regret and repentance for all my past sins by always trying to live my life for God's glory, and by never again being responsible for the taking of another human life.

May the grace and peace of God, the love of Jesus Christ, and the fellowship of the Holy Spirit always shine upon and richly bless you and your family abundantly.

Clayton A. Fountain

I don't believe that he ever received a response.

Near the end of 1992, Clayton began reaching clarity about something he had come to believe since his conversion — that God was "preparing and retraining me for something." Eight years later, he looked back on the process this way: "I began experiencing an increasingly powerful conviction that God was calling me into His service in the priesthood. I resisted, hesitated, questioned, doubted, and fought against this calling. In the end, though, I finally surrendered, and at the end of 1995 I accepted His calling if that is His will for my life." He was realistic about the multiple obstacles blocking such a path, "from varying degrees of skepticism to outright bias and prejudice against me for my past." Yet he believed that if it was indeed God's will, "some way it will one day come to pass."

He would never lose that conviction, but, as we shall see, he began to realize that such a priesthood might need to be confined to a 120-square-foot space. The fact that he finished his college work with distinction and was able to find sufficient finances to begin his graduate degree — these things in themselves are symbolic of Clayton's determination to be faithful to this calling. Although we never talked about it, I believe that the intensity of his academic work reflected the need for this person, who once invested everything he had into his physical abilities, to become a whole person by focusing the same intensity on the mental abilities he never before knew he had. This process became so important that he came to believe that when he completed his graduate degree, "I will be very near my release from prison on parole." He was right, but his freedom would be of another kind.

Clayton's pilgrimage had become so enmeshed with his studies that his class essays are a valuable source for tracing the evolution of his transformation. Two essays in particular from this period are important. The first was a term paper he wrote for a class called "The Ten Commandments Today," which was the third course in the Catechetical Diploma program in which Clayton was a correspondence student. There were several categories from which students could choose topics for their papers, and Clayton chose the category called "White Lies and Secrets." His subject was the "convict code." This code was operative in every institution in which he had been incarcerated, a code "systematically indoctrinated in prisoners, and, in many cases, in the correctional officers themselves." Prison systems are microsystems of society, with their own social hierarchy, ethics, norms, behaviors, laws, and punishments. Operating on the understanding of a class system that is clear-cut and adversarial, the staff and prisoners form "two hostile camps squaring off against one another on a daily basis."

The key values honored by this convict code are strength, control, and domination. Accordingly, the most admired and feared qualities are the warrior's ability and willingness to use lethal force ruthlessly, brutally, coldly, efficiently, and unemotionally. Survival is based on the primordial law of the jungle, in which the weak perish and the strong survive. Prisoners segregate themselves along racial, ethnic, and gang lines, and in such groupings they seek their security. Rule is established and maintained, and conflicts are resolved, on the basis of naked power.

As this works itself out in practice, the operating principles are clear: (1) No prisoner is ever to dishonor or disrespect another prisoner, or to interfere with another prisoner's or group's business or personal belongings. "Mind your own business" is the law, unless the other person is weak. The weak have no honor and deserve no respect. (2) No prisoner is to cooperate with or give information to any law enforcement authorities against or about another prisoner, regardless of what has been seen, learned, or done.

Any violation of this code results swiftly and ruthlessly in punishment with the severest penalty — death. According to Clayton's summary, "the prison environment can be — and all too often is — extremely cruel, brutal, savage, violent, lethal, and dehumanizing." He then testifies that what he has been describing is his own former way of life, in which the military code of warfare and the prison code of incarceration converged as a unified way of life.

Then Clayton provides a clue — probably unknowingly — about the change that began during his total isolation in 1983:

"Within prison environments, all that remains to prisoners is their personal honor and their good name. . . . These are valued with an intense fervor that may seem almost frantic to those outside the prison." Maybe, just maybe, Clayton was startled into asking, "When everything is gone, is there anything left?" Personal honor and a new name?

This is the primal question that the poet T. S. Eliot asks: "Shall I at least set my lands in order?/London Bridge is falling down falling down falling down." Clayton then draws the two-fold connection that his baptism provided. First, he notes that the convict code is "diametrically in opposition to God's holy laws," yet "it expresses the dynamics of prison life, of which I have been the primary example." Second, he confesses in a footnote that "I am no longer part of that code, having become a born-again Christian by the loving grace of God our Father."

An expansion of this footnoted conclusion appears in the term paper that Clayton submitted on February 25, 1998: "Christ as the Pattern for the Moral Life, Modeling the Cardinal Virtue of Fortitude." After "plagiarizing" from his own paper on the convict code, he develops his understanding of a Christian alternative, even for prisoners. Key is a disciplined development of the Christian virtues, which are "habitual and firm dispositions to do the good." There are both moral and theological virtues, the greatest of the theological ones being the divine gift of love. Moral virtues, however, "acquired by human effort and growth through education, are deliberate acts, which are given perseverance in struggle, are purified, and are elevated by Divine grace."

Clayton insists that courage is crucial among these, for not only does it "ensure firmness in difficulties and constancy in the pursuit of the good," but it "suppresses inordinate fear and curbs recklessness." He lists other names for this virtue: "endurance, stamina, strength, determination, perseverance, and patience." In his own case, he suggests, these are particularly crucial in order to "moderate rashness and prevent headstrong excesses when confronted with difficulties and dangers." In his conclusion, he is again prescient about what living out this ethic might entail if he were ever to be released into the prison popula-

tion. The love of God demands a "refusal to betray these commandments, even for the sake of saving one's life."

Another clue to what happened to Clayton is found in the different people who had personal contact with him. Two in particular deserve mentioning. Thomas Brewer, a deacon in the Roman
Catholic Church, began ministering to Clayton shortly after Clayton wrote his essay on Christian virtues. In 1990 Tom began as a
"religious volunteer" in the chaplain's office at the prison. After
Clayton joined the church, Tom began visiting him on Sundays
when the chaplain was away, busy, or unavailable — bringing
him Communion. Later he began conducting a Liturgy of the
Word service in the psychiatric building on Sundays at nine A.M.,
and he would stop by Clayton's cell, spending half an hour in
"meal-slot conversation" with him. At first the two shared perceptions about the day's lectionary readings, prayed, and concluded
with Communion. Tom would be escorted by an officer who sat
beside him, making sure that "for his safety" he would sit at least
three feet from the meal slot. In time, this procedure relaxed, and
the officer would sit in a far corner. Clayton and Tom would shake
hands, and Tom would bring him tracts to read.

Clayton once told Tom that he had chosen the Apostle Paul
as his saint. He felt an affinity with someone who had been in-
strumental in killing Christians and then experienced a shatter-
ing conversion. With Tom, Clayton shared details freely and
nondefensively about his younger life, his family, his killings,
and especially the gun culture that had been his environment.
Deacon Tom listened quietly as Clayton expressed the hope that
someday he might be released into the general prison population (though Tom felt deeply inside that this would never happen). He was particularly impressed by Clayton's ability to tease
and joke with the guards, who apparently were coming to like
him.

There was a time, however, when he became fearful for Clayton. The best friend of the officer that Clayton had killed in
Marion was transferred to Springfield to be the head of human
resources. When Tom wrote a letter of recommendation for
Clayton's admission to Catholic Distance University in Hamil-

ton, Virginia, the warden was angry, saying that the letter was "too intimate." From then on, Tom could only see Clayton in the company of another chaplain. But his concern for Clayton was undiminished.

A second important relationship began in 1992 when Clayton was contacted by Professor David A. Ward, a member of the Department of Sociology of the University of Minnesota in Minneapolis. Professor Ward was writing a book entitled "Study of the Effects of Long-Term Confinement in Super-Maximum Custody." The project began with an invitation to the Federal Bureau of Prisons to conduct a follow-up study of the 1,550 inmates who had served time in the federal penitentiary at Alcatraz and/or its successor at Marion. Clearly, Clayton would be an ideal subject for such a study, especially because of his capacity for self-reflection.

After Professor Ward's initial contact with Clayton, the two men began a relationship that lasted for the rest of Clayton's life. Professor Ward sent Clayton a number of books and articles on the subject, asking that he do a critical analysis of each in terms of his own experience. Clayton wrote nineteen analyses in all, including "Code of the Streets," "On Killing," "The Aesthetic of Isolation," "Psychopathological Effects of Solitary Confinement," "Solitary Confinement as a Rehabilitation Technique," "Reactions and Attributes of Prisoners in Solitary Confinement," "War behind Walls," and "Psychological Survival."

On the basis of Clayton's work, as well as letters, phone calls, and several visits to him, Professor Ward came to see Clayton as possessing "an amazing ability to turn his life around in conditions of confinement that would depress and discourage most men." Ward credited Clayton's religious conversion as being "the key to his new way of dealing with life's daily, and long term, annoyances and problems." In a recommendation he wrote for Clayton, Ward appraised the work Clayton had done for him as being "at a level equal to some of the best doctoral students I supervise." He drew this conclusion: "Mr. Fountain's writing provides clear evidence of a superior intelligence, with an ability to handle abstract concepts and to grapple with complex issues in criminology and penology." He regarded Clayton's contributions as so significant that the two men signed an agreement promising that no one would see Clayton's papers until Dr. Ward had published his book.

As I understand this project, it involved a process known as "desistance," a relatively new and unexplored area intersecting sociology, penology, psychology, and criminology. Clayton sent me this definition: "Desistance is the long-term cognitive, psychological, sociological, and emotional decision-making process employed by offenders in learning how to effectively and reliably resist, cease, and change criminal behavioral patterns to non-criminal, socially acceptable behavioral patterns in order to build and maintain a satisfying and rewarding life for themselves." Again with something of a prophetic eye, Clayton wrote in longhand, "An excellent and original view for understanding monastic conversion."

CHAPTER SIX

From Skepticism to Friendship

———

My first involvement with Clayton Fountain began quite simply. In 1995, I accepted Father Robert's invitation to match the funds that the monastery was providing to help with Clayton's education. I knew almost nothing about Clayton, nor did I need to — only that he had killed some people — but Father Robert was convinced of his conversion. In fact, I knew almost nothing of the life story that I have written about thus far. That was the way I wanted it, because if Clayton was a "new person," I would try to treat him as if he had no past — only an unfolding present, for better or for worse.

It wasn't until 1998 that Clayton and I had any contact at all. Father Robert confessed that he had been reluctant to involve me because "Clayton can really consume one's time unless you put a strict limit on your involvement." Having duly warned me, Father Robert asked that I begin communicating with Clayton because my teaching experience at Yale and Princeton was likely to be helpful to him in his advanced graduate studies in philosophy and theology.

Not long after Clayton and I began our correspondence, Father Robert's warning proved to be an understatement. As I look back on it now, I shouldn't have been surprised to receive a copy of a letter that Clayton had written to the warden asking permission for me to visit him. Permission was granted on January 4, 1999. On January 28, Clayton wrote a letter to me asking if I might like to make such a visit. As it turned out, the very next day he also asked the warden to allow me to receive phone calls from him. I learned of this through a letter from his correctional counselor, informing me that Clayton had submitted my name for such calls, and that unless I declined, my name would be approved, with the understanding that "your name and number will be removed only upon request of the inmate, or [if] the Associate Warden determines that the telephone communication poses a threat to institutional security or good order, or poses a threat to others." I agreed, but only after making it clear to Clayton that these calls should be no more than monthly. Typically, as it turned out, these monthly calls gradually became weekly calls, and "when needed," they might occur every few days.

The next step in this unfolding dynamic was for me to authorize the FBI to check into my background for "security clearance or access." Permission for a visit was finally granted. All I had to do at this point was contact the chaplain's office to set a date.

The Sunday afternoon that Clayton and I chose had a hint of snow as the wind swept cruelly across the expansive prison lawn. The Medical Center itself faces a busy expressway, but as soon as I turned through the gate, all became quiet. A large sign indicated that I should stop in front of a speaker box encased in brick. On the opposite side of the road was a tower where an armed guard was clearly visible. Apparently it was his voice that came crackling through the box: "What is your business?" I explained, and it immediately became clear that I was expected. The voice rattled off a series of memorized questions about whether I had contraband ranging from explosives to electronic equipment. Hoping that I had answered correctly, yet uneasy about whether I had correctly deciphered the response through all the static, I anxiously proceeded. All would be well, I prayed, if the noise actually had said something about visitor parking, which appeared to be on my left. Even with the guard watching me intensely, I still locked my car.

The wind burned my face as I walked toward the impressive

long brick structure, complete with an attractive tall white cupola. The impression was not that of a penitentiary but an interesting merging of Independence Hall and a Catholic orphanage.

I neglected to count the steps, but there must have been thirty. Once inside the small waiting area, I didn't wait long. Questions sent me back to the car several times, the first one in order to re-memorize my license plate number. I signed a paper that I didn't read, apparently giving me permission to sign a logbook. There I was asked to provide Clayton's prison number, which evoked another senior moment. Next was a trip through a metal detector, a request to empty my pockets into a locker, and a stamping of my wrist with an invisible mark. I was now officially ready to sit and wait. Everything was polite, efficient, and mechanical.

Yet, as I sat there, marveling at the scrupulous preparation for my entry, staff and guards came and went, unexamined, through a special door. Within a short time, a chaplain came for me. Together we faced a sliding barred gate. The chaplain waved at the guard in a windowed cage, and the gate opened quite efficiently on its own. When it closed after us, we were hemmed in by a similar closed gate in front of us. Another wave and another opening, and with four steps I was standing before the glassed-in guard. A mysterious signal turned out to mean that he was interested in my wrist. Once it was exposed to a black light, I found that I had been tattooed with an eerie but unreadable insignia. I was told that the design changed on a regular basis. A nod indicated that I had passed the test and was ready for the next barred door, this time with glass.

This one opened more mysteriously. It took me twelve steps to find myself at the back of a seated guard, who finally turned toward us from his task of surveying the crowded visitors' room. The smell of popcorn played unfair havoc with my empty stomach. When the guard's paperwork apparently corresponded with that provided by the chaplain, it was back into the hall again, with access to the popcorn locked behind us.

I confess not remembering where we went from that point on. Part of the reason was that the interior was a maze, but an equal part was my mounting anxiety. All I remember is a series of halls, steps, barred gates, and passing prisoners. Everything that impeded our progress moved as needed — controlled, I was told, through electronic surveillance by a guard who was in another place.

We went first to the chaplain's office, and the two of us became three as an assistant joined us. She had a strange need to relate some of the horror stories from the ever-expanding Clayton legend. I was emphatically warned that there would be a red line three feet in front of his cell door, and a plastic chair would be placed behind it. Under no circumstances was I to lean any closer, because "he can reach right out through that meal slot and strangle you before you can take your next breath." So "reassured," I finally arrived with my chaperones. I took my seat, very intentionally sitting as far back in the chair as possible. The chaplain and the assistant took their own plastic seats five feet away, leaving me unclear about whether they were my protectors or my spies.

By this time, my anxiety had worked its way toward the edge of fear. I hardly remember any of the conversation I had with Clayton, only that the voice that came through the slot was deep, friendly, and relaxed, with a touch of humor. There were occasional hearty laughs from the invisible man that conveyed his intensity about whatever we were discussing. He shared details about himself freely, but his interest in knowing me outweighed any focus on himself. One hour later, almost to the second, my two chaperones rose. Without a word, I knew that my first encounter was over. As we retraced our steps, my chaperones wanted me to understand that the man behind the meal slot was a "smooth talker," so I shouldn't be "taken in" because he wasn't what he projected himself to be.

The shrill wind sweeping the outside steps arrested my emotions. But I couldn't contain them during the hour-and-a-half trip back to my hermitage. I was in a muddle of puzzlement. I could get no clear image of what had happened. Who on earth was the real Clayton Fountain? Indeed, did he even know?

His letter of February 10, 1999, was well-written, friendly, and expressed appreciation for my visit. He was especially pleased that in a consequent conversation with the chaplain, he had been assured that "Father Paul can come again, just so he gives us a two-week notice to get all the paperwork done and arrangements set up."

But this wouldn't happen. Clayton asked me to send a letter of recommendation for some part of his college work. I focused on the positive: Why wouldn't I want to support someone who wanted to improve himself? I sent my approbation to the chaplain's office, as Clayton requested. On March 17, 1999, I received an official letter from the captain notifying me that all further visits were denied. My services as a visiting priest were no longer needed, because "the chaplain's office is quite capable of ministering to all of Fountain's spiritual needs." Any questions I had were to be referred to the chaplain. The message was curt and clear: Clayton remained the enemy.

As Clayton and I continued to correspond, my typical communication of one- or two-page letters would evoke ever-longer responses, often of the two-stamp variety. I would characterize them as reflecting, at first, Clayton's hunger to share what he was learning through his studies. He was intense about this, often reading and writing through the night, getting five hours of sleep in the morning only after he was exhausted. Through the years of our correspondence, I was surprised that I never experienced much dependency on his part. What he was eager for was an intellectual companionship of a kind he had never known before. He had an appetite "to know it all," and he needed someone to help him be sure that he understood what he "knew."

A condensed account of his studies is a significant story within this story. After his conversion to Christianity in February 1990, Clayton contended that "God directed me to pursue a formal education." Although he had earned his GED at Marion, he felt the need to start all over again, earning his high school diploma through the International Correspondence School in Scranton, Pennsylvania. Then he taught himself how to type so he could find prison employment to help pay for his college education. From 1995 until his death, he was employed as a clerk-typist for the Education and Recreation Departments, doing the work in his cell. The work schedule he set for himself was from four P.M. until midnight, Monday through Friday; he initially earned a pay grade of 2. His official record indicated that he was "a consistently good worker requiring minimal supervision in performing assigned duties." By July 1996, he had earned the top grade of 1, with a performance pay of sixty-six dollars a month.

Indicative of Clayton's change of heart is that even though he never made more than forty-one cents an hour, he wrote this to me: "I am thankful, for in no way did the prison have to provide me with this prison job. They let me attain the highest grade of pay just so that I could continue my education."

In March 1990 he enrolled in the College Program for the Incarcerated (CPI) offered by Ohio University in Athens, Ohio — beginning in pre-law with a major in philosophy and business. After his conversion, he switched his major to pre-theology. In the fall of 1993, he was admitted to the Bachelor of Specialized Studies Program through Ohio University, and on August 19, 1996, he earned his Bachelor of Arts degree with honors. He specialized in social science, maintaining a GPA of 3.24 out of a possible 4.0. While he was earning his B.A., he began religious studies through the Catholic Home Study Institute, and credits from this institute were accepted by Ohio University. On January 18, 2001, he was accepted into the Catholic Distance University in the Master of Arts program, majoring in religious studies.

Along the way Clayton earned an ecclesiastical teaching certificate with a straight A record. To get this certificate, he had to complete twelve college-level courses in such areas as the catechism of the Catholic Church, sacred scripture, moral theology, sacraments, catechetics, and spirituality. Among the requirements were sixteen essay papers, a final comprehensive exam, and an independent project. The titles of some of Clayton's essays were "Modern Atheism in Western Society," "John's Gospel and the Synoptics," "The Formation of Conscience in a Pluralistic Society," "Sacrament of the Eucharist by Transubstantiation," "Symbols of Faith," "Authentic Christian Meditation," and "Proofs for the Existence of God."

Understandably, Clayton's letters to me would be filled with ruminations on his studies. Increasingly, he also included his plans for acquiring source materials, ideas for finding money to pay for his further schooling, and creative ways to satisfy such academic requirements as on-campus residency. In the remainder of a typical letter, he would talk about his spiritual practices, reviewing them so as to be held accountable. It was important to him to maintain a viable rhythm between doing and being.

Clayton's letters began to come weekly, usually followed by a phone call. It was hard to believe that someone isolated in a tiny cell, cut off from almost all human contact, could have so much to say — and rarely repeat himself. My conclusion was that he was making up for nearly forty years of interior isolation — both psychological and spiritual.

Other than a modest contribution I made each year to his tuition, the only financial obligation I assumed was sending him occasional checks of twenty dollars to pay for our phone bill. Calls had to be initiated by the prisoner, so while my personal long-distance calls cost me less than five cents a minute, Clayton was charged sixteen cents a minute, with a time limit of fifteen minutes.

As I mentioned, sometimes when I talked with Clayton about a special friend of mine, he would cautiously ask if there was any chance that they might like to receive a letter from him. Sometimes they would. At the time of his death, he was corresponding with about four of my friends, a few of whom were women. In writing this story, I asked them if in their correspondence with Clayton they had encountered any innuendo or language that they would regard as inappropriate. The uniform answer was no. One of them wrote these observations in response: "Our relationship was brief, but I was impressed by his desire to keep learning, the thoroughness of his work, and his thoughtfulness in asking about my welfare as well. His life certainly gives hope for redemption and new life on this side of heaven."

Over the next five years, Clayton provided me with a constant flow of the course papers of which he was particularly proud. Once, when he received a grade of 90 percent on a paper, he had a hard time letting go of his "failure." In reviewing his transcripts, I found that his college grades were excellent, except for anything having to do with math — such as accounting procedures and elementary statistics. His only D was in algebra. Although Father Robert told me that Clayton was given the opportunity to retake the course, he decided against it — keeping it on his permanent record as a "humble reminder never to take anything for granted." Yet, as graduation neared, he couldn't resist proving himself, so he finished pre-calculus with an A. In graduate school, all of his grades were A's.

Clayton's educational successes were certainly impressive. However, because I was constantly reminded of his behavioral record, it isn't surprising that I remained skeptical about the depth of Clayton's professed transformation. A graphic example, keeping this strain lively, occurred one Sunday morning, when I delivered a homily in the local church about guilt and forgiveness, sharing anonymously a little of the "Clayton story." Afterwards, the cantor introduced me to her grown son, who was visiting. Without a hint of friendliness, he pointed a finger at my chest as if to impale me with each word: "Could that be 'Fontaine' you were talking about?" He refused to pronounce the name as Clayton preferred it.

His mother explained that I was Clayton's spiritual director. The next minutes were tense. In the middle of the church, with the few members who remained growing more and more anxious, the cantor's son unleashed a barrage of profanity and anger that verged on physical expression. I took a step backwards, but he advanced. "If you believe that that son of a bitch is anything more than a filthy murderer, you are the most naive bastard I have ever met." Days later, after he had simmered down a bit while staying with his parents, I was told who he was: a guard from Marion who had personally encountered the "Clayton legend."

Yet for me, that legend now had a voice and a face, and in them I heard and saw integrity. By Ash Wednesday (February 17, 1999), I felt this sufficiently to explore with Clayton his thoughts on re-imaging himself as a hermit, living in a cell that he could claim as his hermitage. I might have gotten carried away, especially when I began citing Canon Law, describing the section on "diocesan hermits" who made vows to the bishop and were officially consecrated.

At this point I had gained an interested listener, and my imagination began speaking for itself. I explained how the church year is divided into two "training periods," likening them to spiritual "boot camps" — just to be sure that I was making sense of this for Clayton. These, I continued, are each structured by the rhythms of anticipation, gift, and response — taking on the names of Advent/Christmas/Epiphany and Lent/Easter/Pentecost. I applied this to the concrete way in which for monks these rhythms incarnate each day, liturgically punctuated by what we call a Daily Office. Originally the 24 hours were divided by the Trinity, providing 8 daily times of prayer, at the heart of which are the 150 biblical psalms that Jesus used as his hymn-book. This rhythm renders each day complete in itself, for God gives us only one day at a time.

At the closing Daily Office of Compline (Latin, meaning "complete"), we must hand our lives back to God, as if with the words of Jesus: "Into your hands, Lord, I commend my spirit." Then we are sprinkled with water to remind us that in our baptism we were buried with Christ, immersed in the water of his death, and resurrected with him from the dead. Our death has been "died" for us, so with confidence we can return to our cells, and in the "Great Silence" we "die" into sleep. If at 3:15 A.M. we are awakened by the tower bell, we have been gifted with a new day unlike any that we have ever had before. "Christ has risen, he has risen indeed. Alleluia!"

Apologizing to Clayton for preaching a sermon at him, I ended our conversation there. Apparently Clayton was intrigued, because he shared the idea with the chaplain during a visit on February 20. The chaplain supported the idea, promising to make arrangements so that I could send books on such matters to Clayton. He did, and the general prison policy was made to apply to Clayton as well. He could receive softcover books from individuals, but hardcover ones had to come directly from a publisher, a bookstore, or a university. All such materials for Clayton would need to be sent to him in care of the chaplain.

Faithful to the "J" in his Myers-Briggs Personality Indicator, Clayton said yes to the idea the very next day, deepening his affirmation with three reasons for wanting to re-image himself and his cell. First, he wanted to make his incarceration more spiritual and more faithful to a gospel rhythm. Second, he wanted to give his days a deeper sense of discipline by structuring his actions and conduct. And third, he wanted to give his "doing" a sense of being done for the glory of God. Eager to learn more about what such a monastic-type life might be like, he listed the twenty-six books that he already owned (mostly religious and spiritual) and asked for help in thinking through how his library should be supplemented. "While I hardly ever watch TV," he added, "I have begun to watch mass daily."

On April 22, 1999, as I attempted to teach Clayton how to chant the psalms, our phone call became laughable. After some aborted attempts, he got the main idea, but the result resembled a duet between a bullfrog and a monotone. When he asked me to offer prayers for a terminally ill prisoner, I learned that offering intercessions had become a routine spiritual practice for him. He asked guards and any prison personnel who visited him for the names of people for whom they would like him to pray. He kept a notebook, praying especially for his victims and their families. I sent him additional names and causes of my own.

Clayton's interest in this monastic perspective continued to grow, and on May 3, 1999, he told me he was ready to send a letter to the Springfield bishop asking for official acceptance as a diocesan hermit. I advised him to live such a lifestyle for a year before asking for anything official.

By early spring, I became aware of how much Clayton had begun to fantasize about graduate school. It seemed that a Ph.D. was beginning to function as a symbol — something which, if he ever attained it, would mark with certainty that he had made something of himself. On May 7, 1999, he laid out for me his plan for creating a prison situation that might sufficiently satisfy the requirements for enrolling in The Graduate School of America in

Minneapolis (changed to Capella University on June 1, 1999). His plans included recruiting some of the prison staff (such as the psychologists) to function as instructors, getting permission to hear cassettes and watch videotapes (he already had used a tape machine for his college courses in Spanish), and acquiring practical skill training in counseling. I marveled at his tenacity, for all of these "unlikelies" had to be sought through a tedious process from a prison system intent on keeping him remote from all human contact.

But Clayton was undaunted. His intent was to seek a Master of Science degree in human services, specializing in professional counseling, as a means to acquire a Ph.D. This choice sounded strange to me, until he explained that he was constructing such a program in hopes of qualifying for a scholarship from the National Institute of Mental Health (NIMH) and/or the National Institute of Health (NIH). These were the only Ph.D. grant possibilities that he could find that might not be closed to inmates. Later the chaplain informed him that the plans he had submitted to the prison authorities were "being taken under advisement." Then the chaplain mentioned that he would be retiring on August 1, giving Clayton a hint of how slow the process might be.

On May 31, Clayton slipped in the shower, possibly tearing the cartilage in his left knee. There was some thought that it might require surgery. But it was hard to determine the seriousness of his injury because it was difficult to find medical personnel willing to enter his cell under any circumstances. On the other hand, the elaborate and "dangerous" procedure required to remove Clayton from his cell made surgery an event to be avoided if at all possible. As far as I know, this injury was left to "heal" on its own.

It was clearly with pride that on June 16, 1999, Clayton sent me a copy of a certificate he had received, etched with the words "Honorary Award Recognition." On the phone he elaborated, telling me with an embarassed laugh that his name would be published in the 22nd Annual Edition of "The National Dean's List, 1998-1999." This first real recognition of his scholarly efforts intensified his yearning for graduate work, pushing him to explore more expansively any possible scholarship help, no matter how remote. Some of his leads, as I recall, included the Knights of Columbus, Delta Theta Tau Sorority, and The Word Among Us organization. One by one the rejection slips came back, as his past continued to damn him.

One of his letters that I found particularly significant during this period was written on August 4, 1999. It was a response to one of my books that I had sent him, *A Trumpet at Full Moon: An Introduction to Christian Spirituality.* I had used the Trinity as a basis for understanding Christian spiritual disciplines as pluralistic. Clayton was attracted to the mystic-like practices described under the rubric of "The Creator as Mystery." I had suggested that such experiences are evoked especially by the specter of death — as when one might hear the words "You have terminal cancer." Such an awakening to one's "unfathomable finality" could part a veil, revealing deeper levels of spirituality.

In this description Clayton found a clue for exploring more deeply what had been happening to him. "In prison I came to realize with frightening finality that I could die on any day, in a death that would in all likelihood be very violent, brutal, and bloody — for there were persons yearning to exact revenge for the killings and violence that the 'old me' had done. . . . When you are in a cell at night alone with this stark reality that can no longer be denied or avoided, knowing that you are unable to trust or rely on anyone or anything else except yourself, that's when it doesn't take long to get to the bottom line that shakes one to the roots." He found the word *mystery* useful for what happened next. "My experience was of a source so deep within me that I had not before been able to identify it or name it. Mystery, or the darkness of nothingness, that is what one is forced to face."

What Clayton experienced, I believe, was the primordial foundation for Christian spirituality. Father Thomas Keating recently pointed to it powerfully in a homily he preached at the funeral of our mutual friend Father Basil Pennington, a well-known Trappist writer and speaker. During Basil's final years, Thomas declared, he went through the "divinely inspired pro-

cess of humiliation and the growing sense of powerlessness."
Seeking to save one's life — one's self-image and accomplishments and talents — brings one to ruin. But one who brings
one's self into the nothingness of the dark night of the soul will
find out who he is. Father Keating likened this experience to
Christ's descent into hell — into "the powerlessness for which
there are no human words to describe." It is the loss of everything, stripped of all pretense, so all that is left, finally, is the real
you. No, there is one thing more — the only thing that matters.
One can experience that self as existing only because it is being
sustained by the Divine Mercy.

This awareness helped Clayton make sense of contempla-
tion. He began to practice it, and to his surprise, he was capable
of losing all sense of time, and would contemplate for as long as
an hour. He quoted back to me my quoting of T. S. Eliot, the line
about "having the experience but missing the meaning." I had
suggested that spirituality is the response of the whole person to
the whole of life. And by learning to articulate this encounter into
self-consciousness, Clayton was beginning to name the Name.

On February 16, 2000, he wrote of "an excruciating pain
caused by a degenerating cervical disk." This condition would
become severe, but the only treatment he received was a heavy
dosage of pain pills. In this same letter, he told me he was
pleased that the local bishop had agreed to place three hundred
dollars in his account for educational purposes. While that
helped a little, his real hope was pinned on the major scholarship about which he had still received no news.

Clayton wouldn't wait to see if he would have the financial
resources to pursue his graduate degree. Perhaps even more important was his determination to discover if he was really doctoral material. To that end, he asked Father Robert and me to
write recommendations for him. Father Robert filled out a stan-
dard recommendation, on which he rated Clayton "outstand-
ing" in perseverance in pursuit of goals; "excellent" in self-
reliance and independence; "very good" in originality and accuracy and in written and verbal communications (mentioning his
tendency toward wordiness); and "above average" in research

ability and potential. I chose an essay form for my recommendation, commending Clayton for his eagerness to pursue knowledge, his determination to read widely and to remember well, his creativity in articulation, his fine ability in concentrating, and his capacity to be a prolific worker.

Clayton's hunger for things monastic kept growing. On October 19, 1999, I sent him a large packet of handouts I had used in my teaching — on subjects ranging from journaling to "extrovert spirituality." Several months later, while admitting with a grin that he hadn't yet turned his prison cell into heaven, he acknowledged that "I've certainly learned to convert punitive isolation into constructive solitude, where my personal growth and development keep evidencing to me the presence of our Lord's loving grace and mercy."

On March 9, 2000, Clayton noted in passing that his back pain had been strong and constant for the past six weeks, and was only occasionally helped by the potent pain medication. Then he blurted out his huge disappointment. The National Institute of Mental Health had returned his application for a graduate school scholarship, declaring after all this time that his status as a federal prisoner made him ineligible. Not to be undone, Clayton challenged the institute, asking if they were guilty of discrimination.

In a little over a month they backed down, saying that while they were now willing to declare him eligible, unfortunately the yearly cutoff date for applications was past. Nevertheless, Clayton re-applied immediately, guaranteeing that he would be first in line for the next year. Almost all of his letters to me now contained details of his efforts to find scholarship aid, and to brainstorm ways in which his incarceration wouldn't be an obstacle to admission. By this time, he was narrowing his focus: he wanted to be admitted to the Capella University graduate program.

During this time, I shared my sadness with Clayton over a young man named Jessie. He had been an angelic-looking altar boy, seemingly a perfect candidate for the local church to pay his tuition to a minor seminary in hopes that he might become a priest. Instead, his mischievousness kept getting him into trouble until he was expelled. From then on, experimentation with drugs led him into petty crimes. He was now serving time in the county jail, with little indication that he had learned anything positive from his experiences thus far. On March 14, 2000, Clayton wrote Jessie a letter, sending it to me to forward to him. In it Clayton described the crimes he had committed, noted the time he was serving, and witnessed to the redemption he had experienced. But ultimately he had a sobering message for Jessie. "I know all the ropes," he wrote, "and a county jail can't compare with the big time for which you are headed if you don't come to your senses. Let's get one thing straight. You are responsible for the mess you've landed in, so don't even try playing that 'poor pity little ole me' routine."

Next Clayton gave a forceful description of what prison life is like, shadowed by what for Jessie would be the perennial fear of rape. "Prisons are extremely hard, cold, ruthless, and lethal environments that are governed by the law of the primordial jungle. The strong survive and the weak perish."

After this grim warning, Clayton offered some practical advice. Trust no one unless that trust is earned; keep to yourself as much as possible; get psychological counseling when it's available; make good use of your time to better your mind; and, above all, pray. "Jessie, while I'm willing to help you all I can, if you aren't serious about doing all you can to help yourself, then don't even bother wasting my time." Apparently Jessie wasn't serious. He's now serving ten years in a federal prison. Yet in a recent letter to me, he wrote that he keeps Clayton's letter in his pocket.

As it turned out, on July 17, 2000, Capella University did accept Clayton for the master's degree as an integral part of the Ph.D. degree program in the School of Human Services. But a monumental obstacle arose immediately. To begin, Clayton needed to make a quarterly tuition payment, and he had to continue to pay that amount quarterly, no matter how much class work he took on or how quickly he completed it.

The following day Clayton received a letter from the local Roman Catholic bishop, indicating that he planned to visit. Evidently the Council of Bishops had decided that as a way of witnessing to their new mission emphasis, each bishop would make a visit to a prison in his diocese. This would give Clayton an opportunity not only to talk about further financial aid, but also to discuss something that had become equally important to him. A while back, I had sent him a copy of section 603, paragraphs 1 and 2, of the Code of Canon Law, and he read as well paragraphs 920-921 in his "Catechism of the Catholic Church." Canon 603 reads this way: "(1) Besides institutions of consecrated life, the Church recognizes the eremitic or anchoritic life by which the Christian faithful devote their life to the praise of God and salvation of the world through a stricter separation from the world, the silence of solitude, and assiduous prayer and penance. (2) A hermit is recognized in the law as one dedicated to God in a consecrated life if he or she publicly professes the three evangelical counsels, confirmed by a vow or other sacred bond, in the hands of the diocesan bishop and observes his or her own plan of life under his direction."

Apparently the bishop never came, so on July 25, 2000, Clayton decided not to wait any longer. He made his official request to the bishop, in writing, for canonical status as a diocesan hermit, giving five reasons for his request: 1. "To join the monastic life and the worship of Mother Church so to devote my life to the praise of God and the salvation of the world." 2. "To take another step along the path that God has been directing me, into a positive and constructive solitude within a monastic hermitage in service to Christ, Mother Church, and others." 3. "To serve God by serving others through intercessory prayers." 4. "To follow a powerful feeling I have that, although I know God has forgiven my past sins, I have a powerful, compelling, and abiding sense of sorrow motivating me to continue doing penance for all my past wrongs, crimes, and sins against God, other humans, and society." 5. "To continue striving to fulfill my personal growth and development to its fullest possible potential — personally, professionally, emotionally, psychologically, and spiritually — as a disciple of Christ and a Child of God."

To the best of my knowledge, Clayton never received an answer to his request. In fact, before the end of the year, the bishop indicated that the diocese couldn't give Clayton three hundred dollars for his education, as they had the previous year, because of "the needs of others upon the resources of the diocese."

Two weeks later, Clayton's dream received a severe blow. Both of the grants upon which his Ph.D. hopes were pinned had been denied. The denials cited the absence of any viable training opportunities for practical counseling skills, and the lack of opportunity for an independent research project, given his circumstances. Perhaps most discouraging of all was the clarification that, after all his work in applying and his many months of hoping, these grants were only for those seeking a research career. As a telling afterthought, they noted that no one from within his prison had apparently been willing to write a letter of recommendation.

I DIDN'T HEAR from Clayton for two weeks. On August 23, 2000, he finally wrote to me. He explained that he had been silent because of "the inner confusion and frustration I've experienced over this whole mess. I've felt like I was wandering in the dark and haven't felt up to messing with anything at all." By the end of the letter, however, his amazing hopefulness began bubbling up again. He decided that "I wasn't mistaken about the M.A./Ph.D. work at Capella University being part of God's will for me. God was simply saying, 'Not just now.'" Somehow Clayton was able to interpret the crushing of his hopes as God getting his attention: "apparently He first wants me in the Catholic Distance University Master of Arts program in Religious Studies. The Ph.D. will come later, in due course."

He enclosed copies of the information that he had previously acquired as needed for applying to Catholic Distance University. The cost would be $5,427.24, with a $1,000 scholarship promised. This amounted to a monthly payment of $113. He already had it figured out that with contributions from the monastery and from me, added to his work income from the prison, he could pay off the total amount in four years. I refrained from checking his math, seeing no value in dampening his regained enthusiasm. He also felt encouraged by the fact that while wardens come and wardens go, the present one was dropping by his meal slot every week.

By the end of October, Clayton had begun corresponding with my friend Cathleen, a professor of criminology at the University of Missouri in Kansas City. Not surprisingly, it wasn't long before he asked if he might call her "occasionally." His letter containing the request had a three-page enclosure listing the twenty pending congressional bills having to do with death penalty issues — her area of expertise.

During the ongoing months of letters and phone calls, I found myself increasingly unable to maintain a stable skepticism about Clayton's transformation. My feelings were being changed: I no longer felt that my relationship with Clayton was one of Christian duty. I was finding myself enjoying and trusting him. It was probably inevitable, then, that one day I found myself referring to him as my friend. A little startled, I searched my mind for some clear external evidence that his amazing outer behavior wasn't an internal con job — that his apparent change was more than appearance. In rereading some of his papers, I came to a conclusion, one that could claim to be objective. The direction in which his studies were pushing him, and the intensity with which he was pursuing them, were so esoteric that I couldn't imagine that all this was a front. In addition, some of his work showed an intricacy of theological thinking that was the equal to anything I could do with all my Yale degrees.

If all of this was a carefully executed deception, how could I explain to myself the massive amount of reading Clayton had done since his conversion in 1990? A partial list included Thomas Merton's *Seven Storey Mountain* and *Life and Holiness;* Cecil G. Osborne's *Understanding Your Past: The Key to Your Future;* C. H. Spurgeon's *Morning and Evening: The Spiritual Exercises of St. Ignatius; My Map of Life: The Summa Theologica of St. Thomas;* Annie Besant's *Esoteric Christianity;* C. Campbell Morgan's *Spirit of God;* Bruce M. Metzger's *New Testament: Its Background, Growth, and Content;* Charles Swindoll's *Family of God: Understanding Your Role in the Body of Christ;* Daniel B. Sullivan's

Introduction to Philosophy: The Perennial Principles of the Classical Realist Tradition; Frank Stagg's *New Testament Theology;* Father H. D. Gardeil's *Introduction to the Philosophy of St. Thomas Aquinas;* Father Herbert Jones's *Moral Theology;* James M. Efird's *New Testament Writings: History, Literature, and Interpretation;* John R. W. Stott's *Understanding the Bible;* Lewis B. Smedes's *Mere Morality: What God Expects from Ordinary People;* Robert Paul Wolff's *Philosophy: A Modern Encounter;* Father W. Farrell and Father Martin J. Healy's *My Way of Life: Pocket Edition of St. Thomas;* William M. Tillman's *Christian Ethics: A Primer;* and Austin Flannery's *Vatican Council II.* In addition, Clayton read daily from four different translations of the Bible.

He took his Comprehensive Examination on January 20, 2001, and by February 12 he was able to send me, with obvious pride, a copy of his "Catechetical Diploma." Never one to pause, he sent with it a copy of his formal acceptance into the Master of Arts in Religious Studies program at Catholic Distance University, listing with excitement his forthcoming courses. The heart of his work would be writing forty-three essays. At the time of his death, he had completed over half of the work for the degree, with a 3.82 GPA on a 4.0 scale.

He had already begun thinking about a master's thesis, and in fact had begun his research, hoping to develop it further in his doctoral work. His tentative title was "The Question of Immortality and Resurrection in the Western Christian World: Two Conflicting Contemporary Modes of Thought about Death and the Afterlife." He was inclined to believe in immortality, while I favored resurrection. Our disagreement later made for stimulating meal-slot conversations.

On February 12, 2001, Clayton told me that he had completed a critical analysis for Professor Ward of a fifteen-page chapter in a book describing the situation in Marion prison; it referred to Clayton by name. His response took fifty-two pages. I spoke to him about his wordiness, and some beginning repetitiveness. He was appreciative, and then made a perceptive observation: "I guess it has been so long since anyone took me or what I had to say seriously, or believed that I was honest in my saying it, that I guess I am tempted to overkill — trying to get them to believe that I am for real."

Two months later he likened his studies to "peeling an on-ion, because with each new layer that is peeled away, I learn that there are successive layers to learn and master. Each has its own unique way of keeping me quite humble of heart, mind, and soul. That is as it should be, or else the temptation towards pride and vanity might prove to be too much at times." I suggested that he might also work on peeling the onion of the church's liturgy, beginning by immersing himself in the upcoming Easter Vigil. He didn't know it, but he promised to ask the chaplain for a copy. That way he would attempt to be in spiritual communion each step of the way as our monastic community celebrated the entire Holy Week.

After Easter (May 24), he sent me copies of two lesson essays. While he consistently showed confidence in his intellectual abil-ities, this time he seemed to need affirmation. The reason be-came clearer a month later, when he confused me by sending a copy of a proposed re-application for the National Institute of Mental Health scholarship. Included was an outline of what Ca-pella University would require for his doctorate, and how he would try to assure the NIMH that his incarceration presented creative possibilities rather than liabilities. His suggested thesis was "A Study of the Adult Criminal Justice System: Assessment of the Criminal Behavior, Incarceration, and Treatment of the Chronic, Violent Offenders Officially Labeled 'Habitual and In-corrigible.'"

I teased him about how quickly God's mind had apparently changed regarding timing! I confess that I could identify with the helpless feeling he must have been living with constantly — desperately trying to attain a Ph.D. as proof of his self-worth, in a tiny cell with only the instruments of paper, envelopes, and stamps at his command.

By July 3, 2001, Clayton had cleaned up his dissertation de-scription enough to send it with his scholarship re-application. Looking back on it now, I continue to marvel at the tenacious en-ergy with which he clung to his dreams. Cathleen added another dimension to his integrity, noting Clayton's eagerness for honest feedback on all his work and thinking. Along with several essays he sent her for "critique of my writing abilities, skills, and actual contents," he enclosed a copy of the 1989 newspaper exposé, wanting her to be under no illusion about what he used to be.

On December 10, 2001, he made his first reference to a condition that would vex him for quite some time — "walking pneumonia." What annoyed him most was that he had to stop his physical workouts, a discipline he had maintained since his military days. I'm sorry to admit that I don't know what happened to his back ailment, which had seemed quite serious. He rarely complained, and I totally forgot to ask about it.

Clayton finished his final exams by mid-December, monitored by the chaplain, and he sent me his last four essays required in the course. He enclosed a letter expressing disappointment that the warden hadn't responded to his ingenuity in attempting to resolve the educational hurdles for pursuing a doctorate at Capella University. He also made his first reference to an associate warden who would become a source of major support for him. She asked if the prison's educational department had helped him explore possible Ph.D. programs. No, he told her — he had been left on his own. "Then," she said, "I'll see to it that the supervisor of education pays you a visit." The supervisor came promptly, promising a computer search. Clayton wasn't hopeful that it would happen "any time soon."

As time went on, Father Robert and I continued to see evidence that Clayton Fountain had changed, not only in mind and behavior but in spirit. We recalled three episodes in particular. The first was a story about Clayton catching mice that wandered into his cell. If the horror stories that persisted were still true, he would have tortured them to death, or crushed out their lives in delight with a squeeze of his hand. Instead, he fed them, trained them to do tricks, and named them as pets — until a guard decided on an execution for Clayton's mice friends that he wished for Clayton himself.

The other two episodes relate to a notice sent throughout

the prison that offered a one-hundred-dollar reward for any prisoner who could report anything detrimental to the safety and security of the institution. Soon afterwards, Clayton informed a guard that he wished to speak with the warden. When the warden came, Clayton asked him to step back. Then he thrust a sharp metal dagger through the slot. "Where did you get that?" Clayton handed the warden the instrument, handle first. It was a simple matter, he explained, to take down the metal attachment anchoring the punching bag in his recreation room. The concrete floor in his cell was more than adequate to file it into shape and sharpen it to a fine point. He asked for his reward — and he got it. Then, with a touch of boasting, Clayton added, "With such a piece of metal I could fashion a pick capable of unlocking any door in this prison." The warden showed no interest in letting him try.

Another time, in the presence of the warden, Clayton gently reached out through the meal slot with a lethal six-inch plastic dagger. This time the explanation was much simpler. He opened his hand and revealed a comb on the other end. "I ordered a comb from the prison commissary, and this is what I got." He got his second hundred dollars, doubling his education fund. These two episodes proved to me rather conclusively that we weren't dealing with the "old" Clayton. And the next year, when I was granted the right to visit him a number of times, I saw graphic evidence that Clayton was a changed man. Each time I sat right beside the meal slot, I realized that the Clayton of legend would have needed only one thrust to puncture my skull with either of his "exhibits."

Not long into 2002, Clayton realized that his education would come to a complete halt with the completion of his master's degree if he didn't begin taking more aggressive action. So he did. He wrote a letter entitled "Clayton A. Fountain's Request for Administrative Remedy." On April 10, 2002, he received the warden's response. Clayton had raised two issues. First, noting that he had served eighteen years in solitary status with a perfect conduct record, he requested release into the general population of an institution with UNICOR facilities that would give him the means to earn the funds he needed to complete his graduate education. Second, he wanted something done about the fact that being confined in the Special Housing Unit was adversely affecting his health, causing him to suffer both from walking pneumonia and from a severe allergic reaction to the dust and mold spores.

In his response to Clayton, the warden acknowledged that he had maintained a clear discipline record and hadn't incurred any incident reports for violations of the Bureau of Prisons' regulations for an extended period of time, "yet your record is replete with examples of extreme violence." As proof of the danger entailed if he would permit Clayton's release into a general prison population, he quoted a statement that Clayton purportedly had made to a staff member back in Marion in 1983: "I will kill again." The warden concluded, "Since the safety of the staff and inmate population is my responsibility and my priority, your request to be released into the general inmate population in another prison is denied."

As for the second request, the warden claimed that the fresh-air return system met the standards set by the American Correctional Association, but "a review of your medical records indicates a closer assessment of the air quality in your housing area may be warranted." He promised that staff members would "evaluate the situation."

Clayton immediately appealed the decision on the first issue, reiterating a theme that, while not exactly accurate, would grow in intensity. "In my January 2002 statutory interim parole hearing, the examiner informed me that the parole board would like to see me back in a general population before my next full parole hearing in November 2003. He informed me that my remaining in the Special Housing Unit would be one of the factors the Parole Board would be looking at — for it would count against me significantly and adversely affect the Parole Board's decision about whether to grant me parole."

Two weeks later I received an apology from Clayton. In a previous letter I had admitted that I felt deluged by the number of calls he was making to me. The increase no doubt reflected his growing anxiety over the ongoing dead-end to his educational hopes. Promising to return to a weekly calling regimen, he told me about his latest strategy. The Administrative Remedy System is a three-tier process, involving local, regional, and central offices. He fully expected that his appeal would be denied on all three levels. "When that happens, I'll be able to file a legal action to try and get the courts to order my release from this Special Housing Unit into the general population somewhere." As he understood it, what was going on was political, and the bureau wanted to shift responsibility for any action to the courts. "That way the Board of Prisons will win, either way it goes."

Clayton's walking pneumonia persisted, compounded by an ear infection. The maintenance personnel cleaned his air-vent system, and they were waiting for a part that promised some improvement. In a further denial, the Board of Prisons refused Clayton's request for some form of Internet access that would allow him to address the requirement set for graduate work by Capella University. The warden himself came to inform him of the denial, but he indicated that he would personally contact officials in the regional and central offices to look for alternatives. Another indication of a "changed Clayton" was that he never expressed anger over these closing doors. His word of choice was "frustrating."

On April 12, 2002, the warden bolstered Clayton's hopes when they were talking, dropping a cryptic comment: "Perhaps something can be worked out about earning additional funding that you need for the advanced degree." What he had in mind remained unclear. Clayton thought that it might mean a reversal on his previous request to make rosaries to sell, even though prison rules prohibit inmates from setting up businesses. When Clayton had first proposed the idea, I wasn't enthusiastic. I kept the math to myself, but I figured that even if such an entrepreneurship was approved, he would have to net two thousand sales and hope for tax-exempt status!

The change of certain staff members, plus Clayton's tenacity, resulted in the new warden's permitting me to visit Clayton again. In fact, the arrangement that was made without difficulty was for a monthly visit when I was on the way from my hermitage to the monastery. While I haven't been able to verify this from an independent source, Clayton told me that a special isolation unit had been built in the basement of the Medical Center for Timothy McVeigh, notorious for the Oklahoma City bombing. This unit was intended to isolate McVeigh for life if the courts didn't give him the death penalty. When McVeigh was executed, Clayton asked to be moved to that location, and the transfer was effective as of May 20, 2002.

To visit Clayton's new "home," I followed the same steps I had taken on my first and only visit thus far — except this time my memory was better attuned to avoid return trips to my car. My escort was Clayton's caseworker. This time I counted them — there are a total of nine barred gates placed strategically throughout the maze, each with visual surveillance, including two stations where signatures are required. The total trip to Clayton's partly underground location took fifteen minutes.

When we finally arrived, a guard took us into an office-like area with a desk, where additional prison clothing was stored on shelves. Then he unlocked a steel-plated door that closed off Clayton's area entirely from the rest of the prison. We passed into an empty room, perhaps ten feet by fifteen feet, into which the guard wheeled two desk chairs. Immediately in front of us was a floor-to-ceiling concrete wall. On the left side was a barred glass window with a phone connected to Clayton's recreation area. In the middle of the barrier wall was a heavy steel door with a barred gate that led into his cell proper, but neither of these were ever to be opened. On the right side was a barred window looking into his cell. On the far right were locked wheels and levers that evidently controlled all the doors.

This cell was a visible improvement over his last one. There were two adjoining cells (10′ x 12′ x 12′ high), connected by a sliding steel security door that remained open from nine A.M. to four P.M. during the week, and for four to five hours on weekends. One cell was his living area, and the other his recreation area, in which there were several pieces of exercise equipment. There was a steel door in the recreation area that could be opened into an outdoor area. This space resembled a concrete box, 9′ x 15′ x 15′ high, covered over with steel plates in which small holes had been drilled. Clayton was permitted to go there for one hour daily on weekdays.

At first he and I tried to speak using the telephone, but it kept malfunctioning. The whole scene felt surreal. I was sitting two feet from his silently moving mouth as a faint voice in my ear crackled like a long-distance call from a remote land. We gave up and tried shouting at each other through the glass. When we were both equally frustrated, the guard unlocked the meal slot. This would be our conversation vehicle from then on.

On this first visit, the caseworker sat right next to me, with the guard standing nearby. On future visits, the guard would disappear, and the caseworker would intentionally sit in the corner, reading or doing paperwork. Whenever Clayton wanted to push something through the slot to show me, I was careful to ask permission. It was never denied. For the first time I saw him. He had a full face, with dark eyes, a black mustache, and a mischievous smile. He changed his hair from time to time, with styles ranging from a hippie length to a crew cut that would have made a Marine proud. He cut his own hair, and he liked to surprise me. What surprises me even more is I never asked how this was possible, given the tight security.

After my third visit, there was no reprimand when he and I shook hands through the meal slot upon my coming and going. Clayton's grip was strong. Only once did I violate the growing trust awarded me by the staff. After our aborted telephone lesson in Gregorian chant, I just "happened" to have a tape of monks chanting that I slipped to him. May God forgive me.

His living area was small but pleasant, as cells go. I could see a few things that Clayton prized. On a table to the left of the slot was a chess set. I learned later that he was a dues-paying member of a chess-by-mail club — proudly claiming to be at level two (whatever that meant). Also on the left against the wall was a bed, neatly made, fastened into the floor. On the far wall was a high series of small, translucent windows. In the right corner was a shower stall with a transparent shower curtain. On the wall to the right was a desk, above which were several shelves of books. His chair was a concrete slab fastened to the floor, a "penance" he was later able to modify with a cushion. A bright electric light was always on, with cameras and microphones keeping him under constant audio and video surveillance. Although I thought there was an intercom system, Clayton's favorite way of signaling that he needed something was to throw a towel over the surveillance camera — which apparently brought a rapid response.

I remember the fun we had once when we strategized on how he could have a garden. Since my bringing in a pocketful of dirt would have been highly suspicious, we considered using his toothbrush to sweep up some dust from his outdoor unit, enough to fill a paper cup he had salvaged. Then, with a few watermelon seeds retrieved from a Fourth of July meal, we would have our garden. When our meager efforts failed, he laughingly asked me to consult an agronomist. Although the constantly rotating caseworkers I met were cheerful, and most of the guards were hospitable, their comfort level clearly depended on having the steel door between them and Clayton.

Clayton continued his efforts to fund his education, which was an ongoing challenge. The reason: in 1984, Congress, over strong opposition from the Bureau of Prisons, phased out all educational funding for prisoners (e.g., Pell Grants and student loans) in an act called the Zimmerman Bill. Frustrated by the repeated rejections of his attempts to find financial aid that was open to prisoners, Clayton prepared an eight-page resumé in one determined effort on August 14, 2003. He showed it to me. In it he provided a description of his past behavior and his present efforts at change, then laid out concretely his educational needs. All contributions that might be raised by circulating his resumé were to be sent to me for deposit in a local bank account called "Doctorate Saving Plan." In addition, a friend of mine set up a Web page under the rubric of "Supermax Prisons," making Clayton's plea for scholarships, grants, and donations. Clayton's optimism was buoyed when he heard that he had thirty-three "hits" on the Web page in the first two weeks of its existence.

He waited, but these efforts essentially failed. Almost all the outside assistance he would receive was from the monastery, the Catholic Diocese of Springfield, Cathleen, and me. When he died, there was a balance of $844.94 in his account, with a debt of $2,756.24 for education already received.

Even though it would take him three more years to complete the M.A. program of Catholic Distance University, Clayton persisted in his search for a possible Ph.D. program. He found three universities that seemed to have total distance learning — two in Australia and one in South Africa. The Capella University program meant that Clayton would be acquiring a second master's degree on the way to the doctorate. When I said that this made no sense to me, and that it was also financially unfeasible, Clayton shifted his attention to exploring the three foreign schools.

His research brought clarity. All but one of the correspondence programs for the Ph.D. required some degree of online capability. Since the warden had rejected Clayton's request for an exception to the rule forbidding such access to federal prisoners, he had no alternative but to turn his hopes toward the two- to three-year Doctor of Theology (D.Th.) program in Systematic Theology or Religious Studies offered by the University of South Africa (UNISA). The catch? The cost would be six thousand dollars. In typical Clayton fashion, he refused to give up hope that someday God would open that possibility for him.

Yet his way of "waiting" was to do whatever he could to prepare for that "eventuality." So, while speeding up the completion of his work for the master's degree, he began working on the language requirements for the doctorate. Along the way, he developed fluency in reading, writing, and speaking Spanish, so classical Latin was his next language of choice. I sent him a Latin text, only to have the mailroom promptly send it back, even though I had made prior arrangements. This gave me time to put in place the possibility of Clayton's doing correspondence tutoring in Latin with Father Donald, the patriarch of our monastery, who was an excellent linguist. Through this arrangement, Clayton not only continued developing his language competence, but also made a special intergenerational friendship. Still not content, Clayton began making plans for studying Greek and Hebrew through learning tapes.

As his attention became increasingly focused on his elusive educational goals, Clayton made the difficult decision to withdraw his ongoing petition to the warden for release into the general prison population. "What more could I want," he asked me, "than my own quiet study cubicle, with no cell mates to distract me with television and chatter, able to pray and work as the Spirit moves me? I am a blessed man."

Given the intense activity that Clayton was generating in his tiny hermitage, I hadn't been too surprised when, a year earlier, Cathleen mentioned to me that he had petitioned the warden to grant me "indefinite pastoral visits" of two hours each, twice a month. Apparently, he figured that if I could "drop by" on my way to my monthly stay at the monastery, I could easily do the same on the return trip. Clayton told Cathleen that the warden seemed open to such a request. I assumed that Clayton's excitement over the idea would eventually lead him to ask me if I might be interested in such an expanded arrangement.

I began wondering if Clayton's apparently growing need for my presence reflected a prescience — that he was moving toward a crescendo in which the meaning of these past nineteen years in solitary confinement would undergo their final testing.

CHAPTER SEVEN

Realism and the Dark Night

C layton's educational dream was working itself out function-
ally as a twofold goal — that someday he might be granted a
papal dispensation to pursue the path toward priesthood, and
that he might be freed on parole to enter seminary to prepare for
such a calling. Both goals clearly depended on his parole situation. He had told me that he was eligible for parole consideration
in June of 1984, on the basis of some logic I never did understand.
But surely, at best, this was hypothetical. He did appear before
the U.S. Parole Board in November 1989, but they gave him a
"fifteen-year setoff" — meaning that no parole consideration
would be given for the next fifteen years. Clayton accepted this
decision, content that statutory interim hearings would be held
every two years to monitor his incarceration record.

In 1998, a cryptic statement appeared in his file. It declared
that even if release were deemed possible by the parole board,
the prison authorities wouldn't be willing even to recommend
Clayton for halfway-house placement "due to his history of violence." With such a backhanded imputation, the chance that he
would ever be trusted to re-enter society seemed more than remote. Nevertheless, a statutory interim parole hearing in November of 2001 confirmed that a date would be set around November 2004 for Clayton's full parole hearing, ending the fifteen-

year setoff. By then, Clayton would have served thirty years in prison.

Soon after Clayton got this news, I noticed a shift in his attention, and as the months passed, his expectations grew. Just how high his hopes were mounting became clear when he shared with me that at this parole board hearing, "they could actually give me a presumptive parole date." Translated, that meant that he was entertaining the thought that they might set a concrete date when parole would be assured if he maintained his impeccable record. Since Clayton had no question about his ability to do his part in such an arrangement, he told me confidentially that his working dream was for that concrete date to be five years away.

Such thinking added incentive to developing his financial plan for raising educational funds. On October 2, 2002, Clayton had sent me photocopies of his Social Security card, his birth certificate, and his baptism and confirmation certificates, hoping that they would be sufficient for me to open a bank account in my name, naming him as beneficiary. I was able to open an account five days later with a deposit of $125 that he had sent. But things moved slowly. No contributions were coming in.

Furthermore, it had taken six months for the supervisor of education to work out an "interlibrary loan agreement" of sorts. I could send her any books necessary for Clayton's education, and she would see that he got them. They were to be returned in the same way. She explained the delay in a letter accompanying a returned book I had sent to Clayton. A revision of Program Statement #5266.10 as of January 10, 2003, indicated that prisoners could no longer receive even softcover publications unless they were sent directly from a publisher or a bookstore.

I confess that by this time my increasingly negative feelings about the penal system were confirmed. Whatever prisons may have been in the past, they were no longer "re-formatories." They were now out-and-out institutions of punishment. Therefore, any prisoner motivated toward self-improvement would have to paddle against the current of penal intention. I only marveled all the more at Clayton's patience and perseverance, traits that in me would have worn threadbare by this time had I been in his place.

By spring, Clayton's energies had a clear and immediate focus. On April 9, 2003, he sent me his first draft of a document on which he had obviously been spending considerable time. It was entitled "Pre-Parole Planning Document." His logic was that all his educational preparations would be for nothing if he didn't get paroled, so he had to shift his efforts in that direction. Even so, I was taken aback by what I read. It was clear that his "take" on the future and mine were vastly different. His plan was concrete, including such matters as these. (1) When released, he would go home for thirty days to visit his family. He would put his personal affairs in order, and bring back to Springfield some of the things he needed, which he hoped his family would be able to acquire for him. (2) He would acquire a dispensation from the pope that would permit entrance into a seminary, acquire the necessary letters of reference, and apply for seminary admission. (3) In the meantime, he would obtain employment and establish residency in the Springfield area. (4) He would need to purchase the general items needed for outside living. (5) He would look for a vehicle for transportation to and from work and school. (6) He would continue his efforts to find financial help for continuing his education. (7) He would need a multimedia computer system. (8) He would need to meet expenses for such major items as rent, food, utilities, health care, clothing, life insurance, phone use, and miscellaneous expenses.

Clayton broke down this last category into four sub-areas. A. Wardrobe: He listed sixty-six needed items, from jeans to overcoat. B. Personal Hygiene: He listed forty-six items, from a razor to bed linens. C. Educational/Business Items: He listed fifty-four items, from stamps to a calculator. D. Personal Items: He listed eighty-eight items, from a flashlight to silverware.

My immediate reaction was to gasp. "Good grief, how horrible it will be if they do release Clayton!" When his needs were spelled out with such specificity, it was clear that there was absolutely no way in which he could ever find an honest and livable place in society. He would be out on the streets with no way of surviving — legally. Contrary to his intentions, these preparations didn't prepare *me* for his possible release. It proved beyond a doubt that I needed to pray that he would never be paroled!

His list was accompanied by a pamphlet which provided statistics that supported my feelings. It was called "I Wanna New Career and I'm an Ex-Offender." It described several case studies of creative, enterprising individuals who actually did "make it" in an honest way after being released. There was also a list of organizations and publications that might help. What startled me most was the introduction. It pointed out that the nation's prison population had nearly doubled from 742,579 in 1985 to 1,053,738 in 1994. At about $15,000 per prisoner per year, the cost for taxpayers came to $25 billion and was growing. During this same time, the number of released U.S. ex-offenders nearly tripled, from 122,952 to 456,408, growing at an exponential rate. Then the introduction summarized the inevitable consequences. The Justice Department estimates that 63 percent of released state prisoners are re-arrested for a felony or serious misdemeanor within three years, 47 percent of whom are re-convicted, and 41 percent of whom are returned to incarceration, with 23 percent of these guilty of violent crimes.

Their conclusion echoed my own: "It's not difficult to understand why most ex-offenders end up back behind bars. Once on the street, they face an almost endless series of obstacles such as lack of food, shelter, employment, clothes, start-up money, transportation, and medical services. To add to the problem, most ex-offenders don't possess a marketable skill, are semi-literate, and have no knowledge of community resources available to them." From that day on, my concern became far broader than the dilemmas facing my friend Clayton.

The next day, after sharing his "Pre-Parole Plan" with me, Clayton spoke to his case manager about the status of his parole hearing. All he could tell Clayton was that "they're working on it." Clayton became a bit frenetic, writing to his family to see if they could help him with his "anticipated" release. It was sad, because I knew that their financial situation only confirmed the unlikelihood of the dream for which Clayton was fervently planning.

He quizzed me about what he would need to enter seminary, and whether I thought he might be able to enter immediately after release from prison. He went so far as to write to several seminaries, describing his situation with honesty and requesting information about their programs. Most never responded, but two of them did, writing to Father Robert, who had written letters of recommendation. The responses were nearly identical. "Please shake some sense into your friend. There is no way that any seminary could ever accept him."

On May 19, 2003, Clayton wrote to Cathleen, seeking legal help in understanding the actual status of "The Sentencing Reform Act of 1984." With that legislation, the U.S. Parole Commission was slated to be "out of business" within five years. This meant that the parole board would have to establish presumptive parole dates for all the prisoners eligible under the old guidelines, at least six months prior to the effective deadline. Congress later granted the Parole Commission an extension of five to ten years, followed by another ten- to fifteen-year reprieve. "Where are things now?" Clayton asked Cathleen. He also mentioned receiving permission to have two personal representatives appear with him at his forthcoming parole hearing: Professor Ward and me. In anticipation, he began assembling letters of support from Father Robert, Father Donald, and Cathleen.

By June 20, 2003, Clayton's near-obsession with doing everything right led him to purchase a book entitled *The Perfect Resumé*. "It is imperative," he said, "that I do everything right in applying for seminary admission." According to the book, the most effective resumé was one page long. That presented Clayton with a formidable challenge, because he hadn't yet mastered the art of succinctness.

I had to laugh at his result. It was indeed a single page — with very small print, of course; but he couldn't help himself. He had attached numerous appendices, such as several prized term papers and the results of his three psychological tests. He wanted me to tell him what else he should provide. He was intent on including everything in sight in one gallant effort for freedom — and beyond.

With characteristic zeal, Clayton continued to add to his parole portfolio. As the weeks passed and the growing number of appendices mirrored his growing optimism, I was becoming increasingly uneasy. In fact, I was downright fearful that he was setting himself up for a disastrous disappointment — or worse. I sensed even on his part an unspoken uneasiness, because he kept needing assurances that I would be standing with him during the entire parole hearing.

Meanwhile, he continued preliminary work on his master's thesis, "Immortality and Resurrection," with Father Donald sending him articles on such topics as eschatology, the glorified body, Israel's development of doctrine, patristic attitudes on death, resurrection of the dead, and the idea of the soul — as well as overviews of Plato, Aristotle, and Thomas Aquinas.

The appendices for Clayton's parole hearing continued to balloon, every one of which he sent me for critique. He also sent me an elaborate list of questions, probably obtained from his "perfect resumé" book, about personal attributes, aptitudes, and skills. He wanted me to help him assess what these were in his case. Under the rubric of "work record," he had listed a miscellany: gas station attendant, road construction worker, dairy worker, farm worker, jackhammer operator, food-service worker, hospital orderly, plus his prison industries, which included making blankets, doing yard maintenance, and being a clerk-typist. Whatever the parole board's decision might turn out to be, clearly Clayton was determined to ensure that he wouldn't have to live with the thought that he hadn't done everything he possibly could in preparation!

He had the reasonable idea that the more concrete he could be in his Pre-Parole Document, the better his chances would be. So, instead of just saying, for example, "I plan to obtain residency in the Springfield area," he now felt compelled to have assurances of where he would live, what actual job he would have, and the actual names of those who would provide personal support immediately upon his release. And so he asked me if the abbot might be willing to promise him a job in the monastic bakery, as well as provide a bed somewhere in the monastery complex. I said I didn't have a clue, but I would ask.

For several years, Father Robert and I had been acquainting the monks with Clayton's rehabilitation, asking that they offer prayers on his behalf. When I thought the timing was right, I shared Clayton's request with the abbot. His quick, negative response jolted me. "No way," he said. "Even if we monks were willing to risk having him in our midst, we couldn't possibly impose that risk on our guests and retreatants. Clayton will have to live out the consequences of his actions."

The abbot's apparent fright only affirmed how far I had come, for I felt no fear of Clayton whatsoever. Whatever relationship might develop between Clayton and the monastery, clearly it would have to be predicated on the understanding that he would remain in solitary confinement. I went back to my own cell, sufficiently sobered to pray over my reawakened question: Was Clayton's conversion a sham after all? My abbot was a dear friend, and yet he was one of the many people apparently unwilling to trust Clayton's conversion enough to act upon it.

I wrestled with doubt for an hour or so, on the brink of relapse. Had my perspective on all this been more hypothetical than I had thought? For the abbot, the request was graphic; he treated it as if it were a real and serious possibility. But more important was my conclusion that our respective understandings of forgiveness might be quite different. Perhaps my Protestant background was a factor, but I had trouble affirming that after one is forgiven, a temporal penalty still has to be paid. Penance, if it is therapeutic, is one thing. But if it is juridical, punishment for punishment's sake — that's something quite different. My working assumption had been that the forgiveness Clayton had experienced not only removed his guilt before God, but also entailed his transformation as a redeemed friend of God.

As I sat in the dusk of evening, I became clear about a need of my own. All that I've ever really wanted, way down deep, was to be loved unconditionally. Actually, I believe this is true of every human being. But all of us are deprived of it. From childhood on, the only love to which we are exposed is conditional — "If you do this, then I will . . ." This condemns us to the treadmill of earning loving acceptance by doing, doing, doing — attempting to satisfy the expectations of others. To stop is to risk having it taken away, so that overshadowing us is a sense of unacceptability, of not measuring up, of being unworthy or inferior in some basic way. The inevitable temptation is to use possessions, drugs, other people — whatever suits us — to fill the anxious vacuum.

Yet at the heart of the Christian faith is a God who loves us unconditionally and accepts us as a sheer gift, just as we are. The name for this in my trade is "grace," for such love comes graciously — never for what we have done, but in spite of it. It is in experiencing such unique love in a powerful way that we are changed from the inside out. As Paul Tillich once said, all we need to do is "accept our acceptance." Our temperaments and some of our habits no doubt remain, but the motivational cord that exercises them negatively has been cut, or at least seriously snarled. What the abbot's response had evoked in me was the contrast between erasing one's ledger and purifying one's motives. It's all about being and doing. When our being is changed, our doing changes spontaneously. And so I was forced once again to ask if both of these had happened to Clayton — or only the first?

My uneasiness kept its lively edge when Clayton received a similar letter of rejection from a friend to whom I had suggested he write. This person was the head of an agency serving the poor and homeless. He too responded that Clayton would have to live with the consequences of his actions. In fact, my friend said that he would regard Clayton as a danger if he were to move into the neighborhood where the clinic operated.

I was relieved when, on October 2, 2003, Clayton wrote to me about his experience of these rejections. "I've thought over the abbot's response, and realize that it was about the best that could be expected under the circumstances. I am just thankful that the abbot was willing to take the time from his busy schedule even to consider my request."

Then, as an afterthought, he indicated that the walking pneumonia with which he had been suffering since November of

2001 seemed to have "run its course." What pleased him most about his improved health was that he had been able to resume his workouts. Proudly he announced that he had already lost fifteen pounds; his goal was to weigh 180 pounds, what he considered his ideal weight.

On December 4, 2003, the associate warden suggested another avenue for Clayton's "leisure time" activity. Why didn't he write an autobiography or at least do some religious writing of a semi-autobiographical sort? Clayton responded that if he did publish such a book while in jail, the U.S. Attorney's Office would just file a lawsuit and take from him any money the book might make. Nonetheless, he was sufficiently taken with the idea to write an outline, and he sent copies to the associate warden and me. He suggested two possible titles. One was "Reflections of a Forgiven Sinner: One Prisoner's Journey of Faith from Darkness into the Light of God's Salvation." The other was "No One Is Beyond Salvation," with the same subtitle. In his proposed outline, he suggested dealing with such matters as forgiveness and the Sacrament of Reconciliation, the Holy Eucharist as the mystery that feeds the soul, and self-examination in the light of Scripture. Particularly important, he indicated, would be the themes of grace as forgiving the "unforgivable," learning how to forgive oneself, and living in such a way with "the profound sorrow, regret, remorse, and lingering sense of guilt that one can be prevented from relapse." Then, having in effect put his pilgrimage into outline form, he wanted me to understand the "bottom line" for him. "If ever again I deliberately kill another human being, I am certain that it will totally condemn and destroy me."

While Clayton's sights had been set firmly on the upcoming parole hearing sometime around November of 2004, he was startled to learn that there would be a "preliminary hearing" six months in advance, conducted by a parole officer from Washington, D.C. He immediately requested that I be present and was given permission. Clayton took this as positive support for his optimism, indicating how much the parole board wanted him to be prepared for "the big one."

When this anticipated "preliminary" day arrived, I met the

parole officer at the Medical Center's front door. As we walked through the maze to Clayton's cell, I had enough time to ask questions. The officer quickly stopped me, wanting me to understand, to my surprise, that this wasn't going to be a hearing at all, but a short session to review the prisoner's record to see if he had any additional information to add to his file. This was all that would happen. Having nothing to lose, I asked point-blank about the odds of Clayton's eventual release. The look I received said it all. "What would you think, with five life sentences?" Then he covered himself: "But that's not for me to say."

I gave him a quick review of Clayton's educational successes, which he readily acknowledged. In fact, he was thankful that what he called Clayton's "educational preoccupation" provided the prison authorities with a welcome respite from his violence. But clearly none of this had any significant relevance in addressing the only question that mattered: Can a five-time murderer ever again be trusted around people? As we neared Clayton's cell, the parole officer threw me this one-liner: "Everyone in prison is innocent, and every prisoner claims to be a new person."

On the return walk, I tried another tack. "If you doubt that he's a changed person, I will enter his cell and live there with him as long as you want in order to make you a believer." I felt foolish. My offer fell far short of what he saw as the real mark. Everything became clear when he stopped at the front door, looked me straight in the eye, touched his finger to my chest, and asked, "If you were the warden, would you take such a chance, having absolutely nothing to gain and everything to lose?"

The "short session" had been short indeed. I had been prepared for what had happened, but Clayton had not. The parole officer had read from his prison record to ascertain its accuracy. Then he closed the file and asked if Clayton had anything to add. Clayton sensed that he had to answer quickly, so his comments were all variations on the theme of what would happen in November. The officer's responses were straight from the book of regulations; he made no attempt to make the session at all personal. Clayton grew silent. He knew that the session was over before it started. I felt tears for him, seeing him through the meal slot, slouching like a punished little boy. I wanted to reach in and touch his hand, because there was nothing that could be done or said. The last words were his. He asked my forgiveness for misunderstanding what was going to happen and thus wasting my time. The slot was closed, the outer door locked. The long-awaited session was over. In truth, much more was over.

The wind outside the front door seemed even colder than usual. I drove home, very anxious and very concerned. How would Clayton react to such a heavy disappointment? He was subdued, but if I had been in his place, my hopes would have been shattered. By the time I drove into the cedar forest surrounding my hermitage, my responsibility had become clear. *My task was to prepare Clayton for the final reality — that his speck of space in prison would be his home for the rest of his life.* Given present life-expectancy charts, that could well be another forty years.

The next several months involved a process of gentle suggestion, inviting Clayton to play with increasingly realistic "what if" scenarios. Father Robert helped in this process. As Clayton's fantasies became more contained, his prayers were for lesser miracles. When the time seemed right, Clayton and I began looking at the odds of various aspects of his once-hopeful scenario. As we continued, the outcomes seemed "not likely." I simply didn't know how cold reality would finally settle on him. I only sensed that we were moving toward a telling crescendo. Through it all, however, Clayton never completely gave up hope of parole "someday." The difference was that it was no longer something he would work toward; instead, he would let it rest in God's hands. He would focus his imagination on the slightly possible rather than the unlikely.

Our conversations, both written and spoken, were far-ranging, considering such possibilities as seminary training through correspondence and tailoring the priestly requirements to the narrow parameters in which Clayton might practice them in prison. If ordination were somehow possible, at least he could celebrate mass daily in his hermitage cell, interceding for the whole world, but especially for his victims and the incarcerated everywhere, guilty or innocent. Perhaps he could tape homilies from his cell, and they could be played at masses for the general prison population. He might even anoint the sick, especially those who were mentally ill, stretching an oiled finger through the slot to trace the sign of the cross on the foreheads of those fearful of their own padded cells.

Pushing the bounds of reality, we fantasized about how he might hear confessions through his meal slot, giving absolution to the most hardened murderers, who would be more inclined to trust someone who "had been there." But how could someone with his record be trusted to hold inviolable what he heard in confessions? How could he not be tempted to use private knowledge against the confessees? We wondered if that might mean forgoing all communication with the outside world. He was willing to consider bearing such a cross. As for trusting that he wouldn't break confidences in return for favors from authorities, he suggested, ironically, that the "convict code" might finally serve a Christian purpose. "If I betrayed a confidence, prisoners have a way of extracting the ultimate — always."

Was any of this actually possible? Perhaps, but it wasn't likely. In the end it was a matter best left to prayer. Beneath it all, I saw a mounting crisis coming. Finally it happened. I received a copy of what in hindsight was the most important letter that Clayton would ever write. The date was February 8, 2004. It was addressed to Father Robert, who had asked Clayton point-blank about how he saw the odds of getting a parole date within the next five years — or ever. This triggered the day of reckoning. "That question and other contributing factors," he wrote, "set in motion a chain of events that were unexpected." To answer Father Robert's question honestly meant facing the hardest question he would ever have to face — "just how real and sincere my conversion and personal changes have been over the past twenty years." He entered the "dark night of the soul" in a testing that put everything up for grabs. This happened through an exercise that he called "what if." He would set up a scenario that he would explore with as much detail and realism as he could, playing out the various options as a way of determining the possible, the probable, the unlikely, and the impossible.

He and I had faced the conclusion that very Sunday morning. But his written version to Father Robert put the crisis in his own words:

> In this final mental scenario that I set up, there would be no possibility of parole, and thus the inevitability of dying in prison. I then posed the question: "If this were to be true, then have I been a sucker? Are my conversion and personal changes real and true, or if I can't get out, will I reject them and return to my 'bad old self,' the one that loyally adhered to and lived by the convict code that once determined my life? Or would I remain true to God, my faith, the Roman Catholic Church, and all those who have supported and believed in me all these years?" My Abba, I entered into a spiritual domain that was utterly new and unfamiliar to me — one that had me feeling a bit terrified and unsure of myself for awhile. At first, it seemed like I was out on a limb too far, and it was shaking, creaking, and swaying at even the slightest movement on my part — which had me hugging the limb in complete terror. As I progressed beyond that point, it then seemed that I was walking alone into a darkness so pitch black that nothing could be seen. [I didn't know] where I was or where I was going, and [I heard] strange and ominous sounds and noises that I could not identify. That had me more terrified than I have ever been, for I was essentially "blind" and unsure of myself — something that I am definitely not accustomed to feeling or being.
>
> Add to this the question of whether or not I would surrender my equally strong desire and hope (both of which are strong, fundamental, and instinctive God-given human drives) to be free again one day, or whether I would hang onto it selfishly and fight (or deny) what God may be asking of me? It's difficult to describe with mere words, my Abba, but while I have always faced and acknowledged the fact that there was the very real possibility that I would end up dying in some prison — either from violence or old

age — there was also, at the same time, paradoxically, an even stronger and deeper thought in the back of my mind that continued to desire and hope for my freedom again one day — what someone once described as a "ferocious" desire to survive and leave prison one day a free man. In many ways, my Abba, it was this particular element in conjunction [with] the "blindness and helplessness" of the darkness I was experiencing that made it so hard and terrifying to and for me. Overall, my Abba, this particular "what if" mental game took me into completely unfamiliar, strange, and terrifying territory that left me in what I can only describe as a "strange spiritual state" for several weeks.

I told Father Paul all this during his visit earlier today, but I was also able to convey to him that I have arrived at a much better frame of mind and spiritual state, with my "what if" game more or less concluded. I still don't know where I am going, or where God may be ultimately leading me (. . . and thus am experiencing the "blindness" that I found so discomforting and upsetting), but that is all right, for I don't need to know this. That was, as it turns out, the entire point all along, but I couldn't learn or see it until I had resisted and fought it (which is futile, but humans still have to try doing so) before I learned that surrendering and placing my trust and faith in God to continue leading me through the "darkness" is exactly the whole point. Another equally important point is that while I may continue to have a strong desire and hope to be free again one day, to give it up and to surrender it to God is to effectively "sacrifice" it to Him.

What is the point, or answer, to all this? Well, for one thing, my conversion and personal changes have been genuine, for I will not reject and betray my faith, my God, or those who have believed in me — and return to the person I was back then. And for another thing, if I am to die in prison, then so be it, because that is what God knows is for my ultimate good and best. The short of it, my Abba, is that, paradoxically, I will certainly continue to hope that I will be paroled, yet at the same time I have also accepted that I will die in prison — that this is to be my "home" for the rest of my life. Yes, I know that this is a paradox, but it is true — though I can't precisely explain how. . . . Either way, God has some purpose or mission for me to complete.

Then he added, "My chances of being paroled could easily be judged to be almost non-existent; yet, on the other hand, we both know that there is nothing impossible for God. How different I am now from the person I was when my only interest (besides survival) was how I could make life miserable for the prison officials."

He had begun this letter at 10:51 P.M. He ended it at 1:35 A.M. This intense effort to convey to a man whom he loved that all was well and that his foundation was firm had taken him two and three-quarter hours.

Two weeks later, his letter to me was one of exceptional gentleness. From then on, his moments of excitement tended to focus not on the future but on what was immediately in front of him — in the "now." He marveled over the recent "visitation of two mourning doves who have taken to perching on top of my outside recreation area, the one covered by a crisscross pattern of steel screening supported by steel beams. It is a large enough pattern to more than adequately permit sunshine and fresh air to come through with no problem. They sun and warm themselves for a couple of hours, with a cooing that goes straight to my soul. We enjoy each other a great deal each afternoon."

Then he became more reflective. The most important insight from his time of testing, he ventured, had to do with how the darkness into which he had been thrust was in actuality a spiritual realm, one that was "strong, unknown, and alien." There was a paradox at the heart of the initial terror, so that "the more I fought and struggled against that darkness, the more profound and terrifying it continued to become. But the more I relaxed and accepted and trusted, the less terrifying and more confident I became in navigating that darkness safely." The classic Christian mystics couldn't have described better what had happened to him.

Clayton received an unexpected gift from the associate warden who was visiting him weekly. She loaned him a book entitled *Man for Others.* It was about Maximilian Kolbe, a Franciscan priest who in Auschwitz volunteered to take the place of a married prisoner, a father, who had been arbitrarily chosen to die a slow death in the "starvation bunker." Clayton devoured the book. He had found his saint. This was the one who showed him that "the possibility of my being asked to 'sacrifice' my freedom for Christ is really of no consequence in the overall scheme of things." Then Clayton named his bottom line. "There will be a certain joy in submitting myself completely to His will," he said in a typed letter to me, "and I pray that He grants me the grace to do His will and not my own." Then he added a handwritten postscript: "That is true freedom!"

CHAPTER EIGHT

Almost a Home

———

I t was at this point in Clayton's pilgrimage that grace came in a way he never expected. Several months before, as the abbot and I washed dishes together, he asked about Clayton. As we talked, he suddenly stopped and asked a question that stunned me. "Do you think that Clayton might be interested in a more formal tie to the monastery?" I asked if he had in mind that of "Associate." (Associates are a loose association of persons who meet independently for reading and discussion of monastic spirituality, who visit the monastery occasionally, but who make no act of commitment.) Possibly, he said, but maybe even the status of "Family Brother" — which is the status that I have with the monastery. Up to this point I hadn't received even a hint of any such possibility. The abbot suggested that we pray about it, and we did. After a month or so, we both felt positive enough to proceed.

It was during my visit on February 8, 2004, after Clayton had shared his dark-night-of-the-soul experience, that I felt it an almost God-chosen time to tell him about the abbot's willingness to entertain a request for Family Brother status for him. He was as taken aback as I had been — clearly humbled. He dutifully promised to pray about it. The praying didn't take long, because the next day he sent his reply to the abbot. The letter was four pages long, complete, of course, with several appendices. In his formal request, Clayton gave six reasons for requesting Family Brother status. (1) Five years ago his two spiritual directors had invited him to explore the monastic lifestyle and to make it his own. He had done so, and now his cell was functioning as a hermitage in which he was a "functional monk," already living the monastic disciplines. He was ready for this life to be embraced by "Holy Mother Church." (2) To become a Family Brother would be to complete the transition from a situation of ultimate punitive isolation meant for his destruction to a situation of constructive and contemplative solitude. (3) He wanted a blessing for his present ministry of intercessory prayer, even his functioning as a "peer counselor" with other prisoners through his "pipe code" — a way he somehow developed for communicating with other inmates by striking the water pipes in his cell. (4) It was time for his studies to be blessed so that all of his educational endeavors could be understood as spiritual disciplines on behalf of his ongoing pilgrimage. (5) While he knew that God had forgiven him of his past sins, he nevertheless "continued to feel a powerful, compelling, and abiding sense of sorrow that strongly motivates me to continue doing penance for all my past wrongs, crimes, and sins against God, persons, and society, through intercessory prayers and penance for others." (6) "I yearn to continue my personal growth and development to its fullest possible potential — personally, professionally, emotionally, psychologically, and spiritually — as a disciple of Christ and a Child of God."

He then introduced himself to the abbot by providing a summary of his sordid past, his conversion, and his life since, including, of course, his educational accomplishments. He then asked questions about the process, such as how he might formally profess the three evangelical vows under the Rule of St. Benedict (poverty, chastity, and obedience), what clothing he might be permitted to wear to distinguish his new status, and how he might have his quarters blessed and consecrated as a hermitage.

His appendices included his daily monastic schedule, a description of the seven Daily Offices he used, a schedule of psalms chanted, a list of Bible readings for special seasons, and a copy of the eight-page summary that he had prepared in his appeal for educational funds.

The abbot wrote a gracious four-page response on February 16, indicating that he was touched by Clayton's openness and the trust and confidence that it implied. "Your seriousness and the degree of your self-knowledge are two important qualities in a candidate for the monastic life." The abbot acknowledged that granting him Family Brother status would be highly unusual, yet "that simply means that your request offers us all the opportunity, and the adventure it promises, to set a precedent by charting new terrain." He promised to present Clayton's request to the monastic council, comprised of the senior monks. If their response was positive, the rest of the community would discuss the request, and then put it to a vote. In the meantime, he wrote, "be assured of my prayers for your intentions, and my gratitude for your life." This letter came with two gifts that moved Clayton greatly. The first was a photo of the abbot. The second was the simple gesture of calling him "*Brother* Clayton."

The request then entered that mysterious realm the monks call "monastic time," to which the term "haste" could never be applied. The process took almost five months. Yet this time was the happiest of Clayton's life. What made all this so important for Clayton had to do with a letter he had once written to Father Robert. In it he confessed being hurt because there were so few people who acknowledged his conversion as real. In response, Father Robert reminded Clayton that the purpose of a conversion is not to please anyone but God. Clayton took this to heart. But now he was coming to sense that he was on the verge of having a home, a place of spiritual belonging made up of people whom he admired and who believed in him.

During this same time a new dynamic arose, one that was a bit more difficult to understand. Father Robert had greater difficulty with it than I did. The issue was fasting. Part of the difference may have been that I was physically able to see Clayton, while Father Robert never had. When he was a Marine, Clayton was a healthy 180 pounds, but since then he had gained considerable weight; now he weighed 245 pounds. He was determined to do a complete fast for at least one week a month. Father Robert was immediately concerned, cautioning him against such an extreme regimen. As I look back on the scenario, part of his uneasiness may have been fueled by his experience with a monastic brother who had anorexia and who became so weak that he died. An exchange of letters with Father Robert led Clayton to relax his plan so that he would fast three days a week.

Still, Clayton didn't give up. He sent Father Robert six reasons for his more rigid fasting proposal. The most important was the ongoing theme of penance. "I need to atone for sins committed, either by myself or by others." Serious fasting would be his way of living out a sincere repentance, resolving to amend his life, expiate the guilt and punishment incurred for having sinned against God, and intercede on behalf of others and himself. Second, fasting would be an ascetic deepening of his ongoing formation as a "lay monk." Third, he would be assured that in all of this God was the priority in his life. "Although I believe that God has forgiven my sins, I feel there is a remaining 'stain,' for I know what damage such sins can do to a person; and I need to be kept humble and be prevented from ever relapsing." Fourth, fasting would be a way of "being in unity with the whole of Mother Church." Fifth, on the more practical side, he acknowledged the need to reduce his weight and maintain it at a healthy level over the long term. Finally, he would correlate such dieting with increased daily workouts. With his case made, he proposed fasting for four to six days each month, and eating only one meal daily for the remainder of the month.

My visual appraisal confirmed that Clayton was overweight, and I appreciated his efforts to honor the body as the temple of the resident Spirit. In talking with me about fasting, he had also mentioned his desire to identify with the poor of the world, and to do penance for the sin of those producing such a systemic gap between the rich and the poor. As Ash Wednesday approached, Father Robert relented.

But Clayton's letter thanking Father Robert for "blessing my full fasting regimen" made me uneasy. He sketched out what he meant by "increased workouts." His auto-powered treadmill had been broken for some time, and it had been replaced with an adjustable stair stepper (a Tunturi Tri Stepper 500). He used it for over an hour a day. He also used the walls as a punching bag for forty minutes, did three sets of twenty-five bends and thrusts, ten minutes of combination kicks, and three to ten minutes of "reverse round-house kicks." "After this, I am totally drenched with sweat from head to toe," he wrote. Understandably.

As though this weren't enough, in a second session after supper he did "dips and curls" for an hour, followed by thirty to fifty curls using water-filled plastic bags inside a pillowcase (one set weighed twenty-five pounds each, the other forty-five pounds each). He planned to add sit-ups and pull-ups. This added up at minimum to two hours of intense exercise daily, but it was usually closer to four hours. I cautioned Clayton about his enthusiasm, but I was temporarily resigned to consider such efforts as a Lenten discipline.

Clayton carefully kept the warden and associate warden informed of what he was doing at each point along the way, as he had done meticulously ever since his conversion. He was particularly vigilant in providing the prison authorities with copies of all materials that he was sending to the abbot. Clayton wrote to me about a conversation he had with the associate warden on March 24, 2004. She had expressed hope that he would hear soon from the monastery because "I have a feeling that God is at work here, although I do not know what purpose God has in mind. I just have a feeling that it is the beginning of something incredibly good and positive." Later, Clayton admitted to me, laughing, how surprised he was to have a prison authority as a friend. But now, he added with sadness, she would be leaving in two months; she had been promoted to warden in a California institution.

Her encouragement was enough prodding for Clayton to write to the abbot, expressing hope that he might become a Family Brother by Easter, for "that would be, in a manner of speaking, my second 'rebirth' into the life of Christ." He said that he had been fasting for a week, having only water, coffee, and tea. He was beginning another such week, and planned to do the same for Holy Week.

Holy Week 2004 may have been the high point of Clayton's life. On Palm Sunday, the chaplain heard his confession, commenting positively on how thorough it was; this was followed by Communion. Clayton then asked the priest if he would bless some "perfume oil for men" that he had, explaining that he hoped to be able "to anoint myself during the special events of the Easter Triduum Liturgy." The priest offered the blessing, and encouraged him to ask the prison officials to allow him to have a small version of the Easter candle in his cell. Preparing him for a rejection, I joked that his perennial overhead light could serve as his "eternal flame." After Communion he began his week-long fast until the Easter celebration. During the week we spoke by phone several times, for Clayton wanted so much to be in spiritual contact as the world church progressed through the liturgy. Throughout the week, his own personal litany seemed to be "how much I have to do penance for."

Somehow he had mastered the "clip art" program on his computer, and this allowed him to add simple images to his writing. With obvious trial and error, he designed an eight-page pamphlet, complete with airplanes representing the Holy Spirit. With obvious pride, he sent the result to his hoped-for new-abbot-to-be, to Father Robert, and to me. It was entitled "Flight of the Spirit from the Monastic Hermitage of Brother Clayton." Part of it deserves to be quoted:

> Although physically separated from the rest of his monastic community at Assumption Abbey and from the rest of the Church and other human beings, Clayton Fountain will nonetheless not feel alone or isolated when celebrating the Easter Triduum — for he will be joined in spirit by all the Church, which is One, Holy, Catholic, and Apostolic. It will be a very special Easter Liturgy for Brother Clayton this year because he will hopefully be celebrating soon his "second" rebirth into the Life of Christ. The first rebirth occurred when he was Baptized and Confirmed on Easter Sunday, 19 April 1992. . . . His Family Brother connection with the monastery will be the beginning of

something truly humbling and quite remarkable for him — mentally, psychologically, emotionally, physically, and spiritually. Using his own Missal, Brother Clayton will be celebrating the sacred liturgy of the Triduum at the exact same time as his very special friend Father W. Paul Jones and the rest of his monastic brothers.

With typical enthusiasm, Clayton told the abbot that with his new computer skills he could design a slide show for vocational recruitment and guest orientation. He had great plans, inhibited only by the "temporary" problem of getting photographs of the monastery into the prison.

The holistic manner in which he intended to incarnate the monastic vow of stability as a way of life became clear in his April 27 letter. Following the One who promised to "make all things new," he had asked permission to claim his hermitage as his "permanent" home by repainting it. After receiving permission, he shared his experience as if it were a great adventure. Preparing the walls where the roof had leaked took him a week of monastic patience. Then, with consummate pride he announced complete success in scraping clean a large area on the concrete floor where mineral deposits had accumulated and hardened. After that, the painting itself was "a slam dunk."

He was clearly dissatisfied when he received a letter from a person who was attempting to collect (for publication) data and stories from prisoners exposing the faults of the criminal justice system. "Any human-run organization has faults so that criticisms can be leveled against it," he told me. "But rather than doing so in a hateful, in-your-face, anti-system sort of way, I choose instead to approach the problems more level-headed[ly], by engaging in a process of reasoned, constructive criticisms that are designed to be a part of the solution rather than a continuing part of the problem."

In a letter the next day he shared two concerns. The first was that his nephew had been incarcerated in a Georgia state prison, beginning a dynamic that had the makings of following in Clayton's path. "I fear for him and his well-being, and I feel frustration and guilt over what I have done, making me unable to help him, my sister, and the rest of my family." I was thankful for the way he concluded: "All I can do is offer my love and support, if only by listening to them vent a bit, continuing to pray and intercede for them each day. I am learning not to worry so much about matters that are in God's hand."

He asked my advice about his second concern. Should he file a complaint? In his efforts to make a wholesale spiritual change, he had become determined to adopt a totally monastic vegetarian diet. He began by proposing a sample diet to the food-service administrator, listing as his reasons the desire to be monastic, to be healthy, and to lose weight. But, he concluded, he hoped for sufficient quantities of food so that he wouldn't be hungry all the time. His proposal was approved, but, according to Clayton, the food stewards "have been doing everything they can to sabotage or undermine it." This had apparently become an ongoing contest — whether in irritation over the inconvenience or in resentment at a prisoner's effort at self-discipline, I don't know.

Quite frankly, the diet he laid out was overwhelming, even though he regarded it as the equivalent of one meal daily. A breakfast of fruit and coffee seemed reasonable. But then for lunch and supper, his list included a quarter of a head of both lettuce and cabbage, three tomatoes, two cucumbers, one onion, four carrots, two potatoes, six slices of bread, two dill pickles, eight ounces of fish, eight ounces of cheese, two pieces of fruit, salad dressing, cold pasta salad, and two thermoses of hot water. No longer worried that he would waste away, I suggested that he "cool" the complaint.

Father Donald, with whom Clayton was studying Latin, shared a letter from May 5. Clayton was becoming concerned again about the upcoming full-parole hearing, the date for which was now sometime between July and November. He was also excited over the possibility, no matter how remote, of being permitted to enter seminary as a candidate for the priesthood. In anticipation of that "slim" possibility, he asked whether Father Donald might be willing to write a letter of recommendation that

Clayton could send out as needed — to the parole board, to the seminary administration, and to the pope.

Through the spring, Clayton and the abbot continued their correspondence, deepening the "spiritual bond" that was being formed with the monastery. On June 2, Clayton felt the need to make certain that the abbot understood clearly his past as well as his present attitude toward that past:

> During my first nine years of confinement I was filled with negativity, destructiveness, and rebelliousness. Prisons are filled with persons like me, utterly refusing to accept responsibility for our behavior. Instead, we choose to blame everyone and everything around us for our troubles and tragic waste of our lives in negativity and destructiveness. I refuse to be that irresponsible ever again, for I have come to learn that when all else is said and done, I am totally and completely responsible for all that I think, say, feel, and do. Because of that profound truth, I also refuse to succumb to the temptation of being unfair, biased, and prejudiced about the criminal justice system as a whole, or the prison system in particular.

Clayton was apparently doing all he could think of to make sure that whatever monastic status he might be given, it would not involve deception — of others or of himself.

The abbot rejected Clayton's first "Statement of an Approved Rule of Life with Assumption Abbey." In it he had indicated his desire to profess the primary vow of *conversio morum* ("conversion of lifestyle") taken by Trappist monks, as well as the vow of obedience to the abbot, to his spiritual director(s), and to the warden. Clayton also included following an exercise and fasting regimen in order to "promote and maintain proper health and spiritual fitness," continuing his pursuit of graduate studies, praying daily the Divine Office, maintaining a daily intercessory prayer list for those in need, doing works of charity "as opportunities may present themselves," and providing "an accounting of my financial status."

The abbot responded in a way that seemed a bit curt, conveying the feeling that Clayton may have overstepped his bounds in his requests. As I read them, however, they seemed to be not so much requests for things from the monastery as promises he wished to make in order to be held more responsible for his ongoing pilgrimage into Christ. The abbot indicated that the vows of *conversio morum* and the evangelical counsels of poverty, chastity, and obedience are not entailed in becoming a Family Brother. These vows, however, could be professed as "private" rather than "public" vows, perhaps with his spiritual director. Furthermore, the abbot did not wish to be apprised of Clayton's financial status, or to be responsible for Clayton's obedience. With appropriate "remorse," Clayton revised his "Official Statement of Spiritual Bond" accordingly, and resubmitted it.

On June 16, Clayton spoke by phone with the abbot for the first time, and on June 20 the abbot said in a letter that "your petition for admission as a Family Brother has been accepted by the Council." Clayton's immediate response was heartfelt. "It is impossible for me to adequately convey just how overjoyed and grateful I am. It is quite overwhelming how you and the community have opened your hearts not only to support and encourage me, but also to accept me within the community as a Family Brother. It is absolutely stunning to and for me to be the recipient of your love, acceptance, support, and encouragement. Thank you all, from the bottom of my heart." He then asked if it would be at all possible to have two crucifixes sent to him — one to put on the wall, and a small one to wear around his neck.

The abbot sent further good news on June 26. The community had met, and "they were very positive." The next step would be to let the monks reflect and pray further on Clayton's request, with voting to occur on Sunday, July 19, "if you can wait that long!" the abbot joked. Apparently he couldn't. Clayton Fountain died on July 12. The vote occurred as scheduled. It was unanimous.

The final "Bond" as accepted read this way:

The Abbot and Conventual Chapter of Assumption Abbey, Ava, MO, receive and affirm Clayton A. Fountain as a Solitary Family Brother of the Abbey. By this act, Br. Clayton and the brothers of the Abbey enjoy a particular spiritual bond whose terms are given below. They express and nourish this bond through prayer and the practice of good works under the inspiration of the Gospel and the Rule of St. Benedict and within the limits of their respective situations, the monks within the monastery and Br. Clayton in solitude away from the monastery.

The terms of this spiritual bond are:

— Br. Clayton may wear the short habit with hood provided by the Abbey.

— Br. Clayton will live a rule of life approved by his spiritual director(s) and by the Abbot of Assumption Abbey.

— Br. Clayton will receive the Abbot's Sunday Chapter talks when there is a printed text, as well as other news of importance.

— Br. Clayton will be buried in the Abbey cemetery with the rites of the Order adapted for the state of Family Brother.

This relationship shall be renewed two years after it has been signed. It becomes void and must be revised and reaffirmed if Br. Clayton's present living situation changes. This relationship may otherwise be terminated either by the Abbey or by Br. Clayton only for serious and just reason.

Clayton had signed the document, and I had given it to the abbot for his signature. Clayton would never receive a copy with both signatures.

CHAPTER NINE

Limits to Divine Mercy?

———————

The end came in a way that was as unbelievable as the life that ended. I was away from the monastery writing a book, and I had just finished writing about the story of Abraham's bargaining with God over the plight of Sodom. "Wilt thou indeed destroy the righteous with the wicked? Suppose there are fifty righteous within the city . . ." (Gen. 18:23). The negotiations became heavy, until a signature line was finally reached: "'For the sake of ten I will not destroy it.' And the LORD went his way" (v. 32). There is an old Jewish belief that it is because of the ongoing goodness of ten anonymous persons that God is restrained from destroying the world for its evil. "But for the Christian, negotiations continued," I suggested, "until the requisite number was reduced to one — the crucified goodness on Calvary that 'the world knew not.'" And yet I kept thinking of the ongoing ones — perhaps ten — who ratified this crucified One by taking on his martyrdom as their own.

At that point in my ruminations, I needed a break. I checked for messages on my cell phone, which I had neglected for several days. There was one message — to call the prison chaplain's office — so I did. The message was short and cryptic: "Clayton Fountain is dead of unknown causes." The secretary would tell me nothing more, only that I could call back later. Forty-nine

years old. Gone. All I knew was contained in those four enig-
matic words — "dead of unknown causes." No, I knew one thing
more — the state of Clayton's soul. I slipped his picture into my
pocket and went outside — into the free air — for both of us. I
didn't want to talk to anyone. As I walked, I wondered. Might
Clayton have been one of the ten?

That afternoon I called the prison again, left a message on
the monastery answering machine, and mailed them this message:

Dear Community,

I want to communicate to you what I know about
Clayton Fountain. I talked to him by phone on Saturday.
On Monday afternoon there had been a message left on
my cell phone to call the prison chaplain. Unfortunately, I
did not check for messages until Wednesday morning. I
called immediately, but only got the secretary. She said no
one was in the office to talk with me, but there was a message that they wanted me to have: "Clayton Fountain is
dead of unknown causes." She said she thought that there
would be an autopsy, but I could call back in the afternoon when the Chaplain would be available.

When I did, the Chaplain said that Clayton was
found Monday morning, July 12, in his bed, dead of an
apparent heart attack. His family had accepted his body,
and it was sent. I asked if they were only doing this to
avoid having his body disposed of in a nameless grave. If
so, I would be honored to receive his body on behalf of
the monastery, as was indicated in the bond the abbot
worked out with Clayton. I was prepared to pay any expenses involved myself.

The Chaplain said that the Privacy Act would not let
me have the names or even the state location of the rela-
tives. But he expressed willingness to call and tell them of
our interest in Clayton's remains. Please ask them to call
me today, I requested, because I wished to talk to them
about the Clayton I knew. I thought they needed to know

that the person whom they had experienced as being a savage blot on the family name had become a redeemed and beautiful person, forgiven and touched by grace. They have not called.

I am sad, as I had hoped for some kind of adequate closure. I know that the most important event in Clayton's life was his acceptance by you as a Family Brother. He wanted so much to receive and wear the garment that was to be sent, and to use the Breviary that you gave him as a gift. Unfortunately, due to a mix-up in the postal room, both were returned to you — so Clayton was never able to have them.

I know that Clayton wanted to be buried with us, but the thought of death was so far from his mind that he had not yet made any arrangements with the authorities or family to put his request in writing.

As you know, Clayton kept sending me the little bit of money that he had made typing, plus contributions from the monastery and from me — so that he would not be tempted to use it for anything but his education. I have put it in a bank account, with the present balance of $844.94. Had his family called, I would have ascertained their financial situation. If I do not hear, however, I feel certain that Clayton would have liked to purchase a gift for the Abbey so that he could be remembered. I ask that all of you give this some thought. What do we need that would serve to honor and help us remember our brother whom none of you will ever see — in this life. I was glad that we promised him burial in our monastic cemetery on the hill, so that he and I could be brothers in death too.

I shall miss him. He will always be for me a testimony to the heart of the gospel: that though our sins are as scarlet, God can and will make us as white as snow. Whatever we do, St. Paul is right — that "nothing can separate us from the love of Christ." Even though there may be none other than us who believe that Clayton actually underwent an authentic conversion, let us celebrate him as one

of God's masterpieces of redemption. May his memory be
a symbol of the power of God to make all things new.

He truly was my brother in Christ, as are you.

Fr. Paul

I forgot to tell the community that I had asked the chaplain
for the privilege of sorting through Clayton's possessions, at
least for something to remember him by. The response: "They
are already boxed and sent to next of kin." As it turned out, he
never asked the family to call me. All I wanted to know was if
someone else besides us, a few solitary monks, loved him. Short
of that, I needed to tell his mother that Clayton A. Fountain died
as a son of whom she could be very proud.

Father Robert had boxed up for Clayton a set of computer
tapes containing a Bible dictionary and a full course in Hebrew.
Now it would never be sent. The abbot had sent Clayton a four-
volume breviary so that his worship seven times a day would be
identical with that of the monastery and the wider church. It was
returned. A waist-length monk's habit had been sent as a spiritual cloak to cover Clayton's prison garb, symbolizing his new
status. Due to a "mix-up" in the prison mailroom, he never received it. I had been given permission to bless Clayton's hermitage cell with holy water. It would never happen.

A week later, I made a final effort at closure. I wrote a letter to
the warden asking permission to visit Clayton's cell one last
time, to step into it for the first time, only for a moment, just to
remember my brother's hermitage home and to pray for him. A
prompt letter in response denied the request, stating brusquely
that for me to do so would pose "a security risk." Clearly they had
already closed the cover on the "Clayton Fountain Story."

During the year that followed, Father Robert and I spent intimate time together revisiting episodes of that story, hoping to
gain some closure. He shared an uneasiness that he had had for
the last ten years about what might have happened if Clayton
had been released into the general population. "My concern," he
told me, "was that the uncontrollable anger he used to have

might quickly be triggered." But I pointed out that never once in all of my contacts with him did I ever experience him raising his voice, expressing anger, swearing, or saying anything derogatory about anyone, past or present. Perhaps, I suggested, he dissipated his latent anger through strenuous exercise. Or maybe the remedy was deeper. Father Robert thought for a while, and then conceded. He was able to recall only one time when Clayton showed a hint of his former anger. His mother called, involved in some sort of emergency. Somehow the switchboard failed to inform him, and the warden refused to let him call her back. He hit the steel door with his fist.

I was uneasy for a different reason. Clayton had made enemies in the prison system, prisoners and guards alike, who would likely have been willing to risk much to have their revenge. Clayton had shared with me how daunting it was to think of all the people who wanted him dead. He knew firsthand how relentlessly effective the "prisoner's code" could be. The analogy that came to my mind was that of Billy the Kid. They both were walking legends. Billy tried to move beyond his reputation as a "gunslinger," but people wouldn't let him. Wherever he went, there was someone eager to "test" how good he really was. Clayton and I talked about this. He told me how it used to be when his life was ruled by training, temperament, and the prison code. If a fight started, "it was him or me, all the way." He didn't need a six-shooter — he had his hands.

With conviction he declared how different things were now: "I couldn't dare let myself get involved in a fight or even a misunderstanding — nothing." "Could you just walk away?" I asked.

"I don't think they would let me," he answered. "As a Christian, 'him or me' would now have to mean 'me.' The odds are good that if they ever let me leave my cell, I would be walking into my death."

He thought he was ready — but who, he asked, can ever be sure? I wondered out loud if there would ever have been any possibility for him to start over again in the outside world, anywhere, any time.

Father Robert and I recalled little things. "What I remember," he offered, "is a man who, instead of becoming bitter, gave thanks daily for having been placed in a hermitage of solitary confinement."

The memory I offered was the time Clayton wanted me to find him a slide rule. "What do you need that for?" I asked. "You have a calculator."

"I always wanted to figure out how they work," he answered.

I got him one, and he did figure it out. I remembered his grin the next Sunday as he showed me how it functioned.

Father Robert remembered Clayton's keen sense of humor, and I recalled his rapport with guards and prison personnel. I only met one who didn't like him; but I never met any who thought that he would ever leave in any other way than a hearse. They were right.

Finally I asked, "How do you feel now that he's dead?"

"I'm glad that he finally escaped — his way, not theirs," Father Robert responded. "He's home now; he's happy. He is much better off."

I understood what Father Robert meant, but our theologies are different. Once he suggested this as our basic difference. "I can't wait to go home," he said, "but you want to savor the strawberries along the path." He was right. I want those berries — with cream! I'm seventy-four, so I've tasted a lot. But forty-nine? Clayton was only beginning to acquire the taste.

I have walked in the monastic cemetery several times since Clayton's death, imagining what his funeral would have been like. I'm sad that he and we were robbed of that finality. I miss him. I wish I had a place to go for remembering.

One fall morning I sat on a bench beside the grave of my monk brother Christopher. I remembered his funeral as if in tribute for what Clayton's would have been like. I was blessed because I was able to be with Brother Christopher during his last few hours. When the end neared, the bell in the tower tolled. The community gathered. The abbot gave him last rites, and viaticum as "food for the journey" through the "valley of the shadow of death." Then Brother Christopher left us, as gently as he had lived. Each night at Compline we all pray for "a restful night and a peaceful death." Brother Christopher's prayer had been answered in the affirmative.

As I held him, like a pietà, several monks washed his body. He deserved a clean habit, complete with the best pair of second-hand shoes that we could find in the storeroom. We brought his body on a bier into the church, and carefully placed it in front of the altar. There his body would remain by the light of the huge Easter candle until morning. After praying Vespers there with him, the community gathered in the Chapter Room, where our somberness became punctuated with laughter as we shared our favorite Brother Christopher stories. Following Compline, we took turns sitting with his body throughout the night, reading or chanting the psalms that he knew by heart.

Early the next morning was his "mass of the resurrection." Then, as we chanted a psalm, the solemn procession began, slowly moving out the rear door of the church, down the walkway, and into the cemetery. Brother Christopher's body was taken from the bier and carefully lowered into the grave. As a final act, the monk receiving his body pulled the hood down over Chris's face. There was no coffin — only the dirt from which we all come. Then each monk took a turn, shoveling dirt into the grave as if tucking Chris in for a well-deserved sleep — beginning at his feet and moving toward his head. I remember closing my eyes. It was painful, yet I shoveled dirt onto his hooded face, a mischievous face I remember well. Every Ash Wednesday we are anointed with ashes and special words: "From dust you have come, and to dust you shall return." So it was, and so it is — the circle completed.

For a month we remembered Brother Chris with flowers at his place in the refectory. After that we continued to pray at his grave, and the graves of our other brothers, as each of us in turn will join them. Love is such a rare and precious thing, so fragile. When it is present, there isn't much difference between a prison cell in solitary confinement and a monastic cell in a tiny monastery on an Ozark hill. For one, there are the sounds of the lonely insane; for the other, the coyotes wail after midnight at the infinite loneliness. It is in tasting our nothingness that our gratitude is born — for the little we have, for the short time we are privileged to hold it, with open hands.

*　　*　　*

EVEN DAVID FREEMAN, one of Clayton's eight lawyers, acknowledged to the U.S. Parole Commission that if all we had to go on was the Clayton Fountain up to 1983, their conclusion would be easy — "that he was a human being possessed of absolutely no redeeming social value." U.S. prosecuting attorney Frederick Hess fully concurred, declaring after Clayton's final murder that he was "the most dangerous man in the Bureau of Prisons," and that there was "no value in the preservation of his life." He spoke with a relentless legal logic. Six years later, Clayton's defense attorney, on the basis of Clayton's changed behavior, pleaded for someone in the system to "take a chance." Those six years were only the beginning of Clayton's transformation, yet during the fifteen years that followed, no one in authority ever took the chance. Perhaps no one ever could.

Looking back on the whole of Clayton's story, admittedly seeing it from the vantage point of a monastery in the Ozark hills, I am sure of one thing. What a tragedy it would have been if society had executed Clayton Fountain on his downward spiral, stamping out forever the possibility of his incredible pilgrimage on the upward slope. The most basic of human questions, perhaps, is this: *Are there limits to God's mercy?* Clayton Fountain taught me the answer: *No. Absolutely none.*

Saint Paul, himself a person "of much evil," intent on inflicting violence, "breathing threats and murder" (Acts 9:1), was brought to helplessness over his own behavior. "I do not understand my own actions. For I do not do what I want, but I do the very thing I hate. . . . Who will deliver me from this body of death?" (Rom. 7:15, 24). Imprisoned within himself, he was transformed by an experience outside himself that knocked him helplessly to the ground. From then on, he was able to face whatever threats came, assured "that neither death, nor life, nor angels, nor principalities, nor things present, nor things to come, nor powers, nor height, nor depth, nor anything else in all creation, will be able to separate us from the love of God in Christ Jesus our Lord" (Rom. 8:38-39).

Having walked the last nine years of Clayton's pilgrimage with him, I have no choice but to stand resolutely against the death penalty — for anyone, anytime, anywhere. His reversal makes it clear to me that the execution of any human being for any reason is the insolent behavior of humans playing god, imposing limits on the God of Infinite Mercy. I give thanks that, in Clayton's time, the federal death penalty had not yet been instituted. *Now it has.*

Epilogue: A Closure

I had thought that the Clayton story was finished. But one quiet fall evening, the phone in my hermitage rang. A southern drawl inquired if I were the Father Paul who was Clayton Fountain's best friend. I had no idea how to answer, or even whether I should. The person on the other end of the line turned out to be Stacey, Clayton's favorite cousin, with whom, it turned out, he had shared much as a child. My questions poured out. No, Clayton hadn't been abandoned by his family. Rather, she said, the authorities had abandoned them, refusing to give them permission to visit him during these years. "I would never have been afraid to enter his cell, but they kept changing their minds each time that I scraped together enough money to be able to come."

Given the family's Baptist background, her questions of me were understandable. What is a monastery? What are monks like? This was her way of gaining assurance that Clayton's spiritual well-being had not been in the hands of some sort of sect. "Actually," she confessed, "from his letters we could tell that he had come home, but we were curious — and thankful."

Then she said something quite disconcerting. "They told us when they called that Clayton died of a massive heart attack, and that he had a heart condition."

"But they never told Clayton," I almost screamed. Father

117

Robert later concurred, with a rare touch of anger: "I really feel it was *criminal* negligence if they never told him he had a weak heart — letting him do hours of strenuous exercise daily, as well as serious fasting."

On May 15, 2005, this same cousin sent me a letter of thanks for clearing up the details. "I can see that you miss Clayton as much as we do. I hope the family contact has helped you as much as it has helped our family." She ended with a promise of, and a request for, prayers.

Less than an hour after I read her letter, she called again. "I've talked to Clayton's mother about having found you. Would you call her if I gave you her number?" I called, feeling uneasy — but there was no need for that. Ruth and I shared, and cried, as if we were longtime friends. "All I ever wanted was to be able to hold his hand again," she said, "but they wouldn't let me." What I most wanted to know was where Clayton was buried. "You will be glad to know that we got a Catholic priest to do a graveside service for me and the family." I was pleased, but something else she told me was more important. "Clayton wrote me once that he was willing to be buried near his father, for God had helped him to be reconciled. We bought a plot at the foot of Raleigh's grave. That is where Clayton's body is."

She asked if I would call the priest who did the service for Clayton.

I thought that strange until I asked, "Did he know about Clayton's history?"

"Not really," she replied in a subdued whisper, "but he'll understand when you talk to him."

*   *   *

I HAPPENED TO BE AWAY from the monastery when "it" happened. When I returned, a monk greeted me: "Go to the cemetery. You'll be pleased." So I was. It was spring, the trees lush, the birds eager. Along the side of the cemetery where the land slopes down toward the stream and its waterfalls, there was a new white cross joining all the rest. But it bore a special name — Clayton A.

Fountain. The abbot had authorized a symbolic grave as a place for remembering.

A week before the first anniversary of Clayton's death, the abbot asked me to prepare a liturgy for blessing that special place. We chose the day before the anniversary in order to give it an added import. We have a picnic once a year, usually on Independence Day. This year the abbot was going to be away, so the picnic was scheduled a week later. We had Clayton's liturgy in the morning, and the cookout at noon. Clayton would have loved it — horseshoes and all.

The monks gathered in the cemetery that morning after Eucharist, circling the white cross. Our simple blessing began with a statement:

> We gather here to bless this symbolic gravesite in our cemetery, that it may serve as a symbol of our covenant with Clayton Fountain, whom we accepted as a Family Brother of Assumption Abbey. He died unexpectedly on July 12, 2004, before he had an opportunity to make known to his family and the authorities his desire to be buried here with us. Yet there is joy in the fact that he had previously expressed to his family a willingness to be buried near the grave of his father, symbolizing an important reconciliation. This has been done in Georgia, the funeral conducted by a Roman Catholic priest.
>
> Clayton's statement in submitting his request to be a Family Brother is particularly important as we bless this grave. He said, "All I have to offer is to be a witness: that if you will have me, by far the least worthy of any who ever dared to ask, may my grave be a living declaration that no person is beyond the forgiving and reconciling mercy of God in Jesus Christ."
>
> And so may this grave marker be such a witness to those who pause before it, but mostly to us who will one day rest in this place — that though our sins be as scarlet, we shall be washed whiter than snow. And so, asks St. Paul, "what shall we say to these things? If God is for us,

who is against us? He who did not spare his own Son, but gave him up for us all, will he not with him also give us everything else? Who shall bring any charges against God's elect? It is God who justifies; who is to condemn? Who shall separate us from the love of Christ? Shall tribulation, or distress, or persecution, or famine, or nakedness, or peril, or sword? . . . No, in all these things we are more than conquerors through him who loved us."

In contrast to my own choked-up voice, the abbot's melodious tenor voice chanted the lead in Psalm 51:

Have mercy on me, God, in your kindness.
In your compassion blot out my offense.
O wash me more and more from my guilt
and cleanse me from my sin.

[Our response:] Have mercy on me, God, in your kindness.

My offenses truly I know them;
my sin is always before me.
Against you, you alone, have I sinned;
what is evil in your sight I have done. . . .

Have mercy on me, God, in your kindness.

Indeed you love truth in the heart;
then in the secret of my heart teach me wisdom.
O purify me, then I shall be clean;
O wash me, I shall be whiter than snow. . . .

Have mercy on me, God, in your kindness.

A pure heart create for me, O God;
put a steadfast spirit within me.
Do not cast me away from your presence,
nor deprive me of your Holy Spirit. . . .

Have mercy on me, God, in your kindness.

O rescue me, God, my helper,
and my tongue shall sing out your goodness. . . .
My sacrifice, a contrite spirit,
a humble, contrite heart you will not spurn.

Have mercy on me, God, in your kindness.

The prayer of blessing followed:

Lord Jesus Christ, by your three days in the tomb, you hallowed the graves of all who believe in you, and so made the grave a sign of forgiveness and of hope in your promise of resurrection. Bless now this place, that our brother who sleeps in peace will be awakened in glory, for you are the resurrection and the life. Then he will see you face to face, and in your light will he see light and know your splendor, for you live and reign forever and ever. Amen.

The cross and the ground were sprinkled, then us, and sealed by the dismissal:

Eternal rest grant unto him, O Lord. And let perpetual light shine upon him. May he rest in peace. And now may almighty God bless us, the Father, and the Son, and the Holy Spirit.

The second blessing that followed was "sinful." We broke our vegetarian tradition with hot dogs — followed by such lesser "sins" as baked beans, watermelon, and a final toast to Clayton, with upraised cans of beer and soda. Amen.

On May 4, 2005, I received a "Dearest Fr. Paul" letter from Ruth, basically as thanks for "your deep love and understanding of my son." She asked for prayers "to guide me and my other children as we try to find solace in all this. But I find myself at times still wondering about the circumstances of his death." On a lighter note, she described with obvious pleasure a dinner her children had to celebrate her sixty-sixth birthday. Then she returned to her loss. "Perhaps his death came when God finally said, 'Clayton, you have paid all that is necessary for your crimes, and so I am placing your life in my keeping. I have a better place for you. Enough is enough.'"

In a subsequent phone conversation, she was able to ask the question that had haunted her for so many years. "Am I deluded to the point of wanting to believe that he became a different man?" There was a long pause. Taking a deep breath, she finished. "I don't think so. It is my firm belief that my son had truly turned his life to God."

Her letter of July 23, 2005, finally brought the closure I needed. I had sent her a copy of the liturgy of blessing we had prepared to use the day before the first anniversary of his death. "Thanks to the whole community for your loving tribute to Clayton," she wrote. "My daughters and I went to his grave and placed fresh flowers there, reading the service that you used. We did it at the same time as you." She closed her letter with these words. "Clayton's death took an awful lot from me. Never does a day go by without me praying and talking to God and to Clayton's picture. A mother's heart can be broken just so many times. Only prayer and faith in God give me the strength to carry on."

There was a postscript. "The family discussed the writing of the life of Clayton, especially of his conversion and how he devoted his years to God after all he had done. We feel that you are the one who knew him best, and thus are the only one who can authenticate his conversion and his faith." I had not previously thought of doing so.

*   *   *

"The dignity of human life must never be taken away, even in the case of someone who has done great evil."

Pope John Paul II, 1999